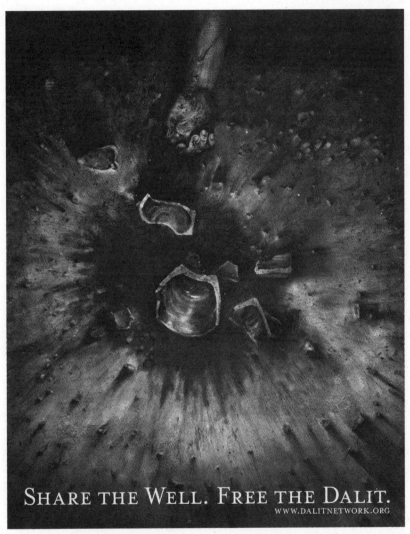

SHARE THE WELL. FREE THE DALIT.

WWW.DALITNETWORK.ORG

Artwork courtesy of Christopher Koelle, Portland Studios, Inc.

Now and Forever

The Epic Struggle for Dalit Emancipation

"I don't have words to express how important I think this book is. I believe it is one of the greatest challenges facing the Church around the world at this time. Please get extra copies to give to friends and PLEASE get involved in the Dalit Freedom Network. Let's also mobilize prayer for this situation."

George Verwer, Founder, OM International

"Some 250 million people in India are denied their basic human rights and dignity. Oppressed and downtrodden, the Dalits of India are experiencing increasing atrocities. It is time for the Church to act.

"This is the central message of this powerful book written from the unique perspective of a Christian leader who has become an international advocate for the Dalits. Dr. D'souza presents a coherent and compelling case for Christian involvement in this critical human rights issue beginning with a well documented historical analysis of the plight of the Dalits and their first steps towards emancipation. With personal stories he draws the reader deeply into the lives of these precious people, so broken by the caste system. Dr. D'souza leaves us in no doubt that our responsibility to act is a question of moral duty underpinned by a Christian worldview of equality.

"*Dalit Freedom - Now and Forever* is a manifesto for change to seek equality and redress for the Dalits. Remember, whatsoever is done unto the least of these is done unto Him."

Tina Lambert, Advocacy Director/Deputy National Director
Christian Solidarity Worldwide

"It was a beautiful March morning and I found myself in a very unique situation. I was sitting in the office of a film director talking about the state of American culture and the power of film. Since I work as an executive in the film industry, this might not seem so unique. What made it unique for me was the fact that I was in Bombay, India. My good friend Joseph D'souza had arranged the meeting as part of a trip my family and I were taking to India to see the plight of the Dalits and the work of the Dalit Freedom Network.

"Over the last few years I have had the privilege of getting to know Joseph, both as a leader in India, and as a personal friend. He is an exceptional human being who is being used in a mighty way to see his nation transformed for the cause of truth and righteousness. The pages you read here will give you some idea of how articulate and informed Joseph is regarding the political and spiritual condition of India and what needs to be done to cooperate with the movement of God's Spirit in these amazing times."

Dr. Bob Beltz , President, The Telos Project
Teaching pastor, author, conference speaker

"In the context of a post-Durban UN conference against caste and racial discrimination, the work done by Dr. D'souza and the committed team that works within organizations like the AICC, the Dalit Freedom Network and various other groups, has brought about a sea of change in the understanding of Western societies, states, media, and more particularly the Church.

"This small manifesto that Dr. D'souza has written helps the world understand his position on the question of religious freedom for Dalits, Tribals and OBCs, and also the role of the Church. It brings out the history of struggles endured by the oppressed masses of India and works out a program for liberation of the untouchable and oppressed communities in India. In the future, the campaigns of global human rights leaders, whether religious or secular, should focus on the abolition of untouchability and caste discrimination in India."

Dr. Kancha Ilaiah, Professor, Osmania University;
Author, Why I am Not a Hindu

"This book is a call for the USA and other Western nations to insist on true progress, development and growth in the Two-thirds world. This will mean a global movement that works to end the caste discrimination and oppression that exists in different levels of society in India and around the world. The Dalits of India must find full socio-spiritual emancipation and empowerment in this generation."

Dr. Udit Raj, President, Justice Party; Chairman, All India
Confederation of Scheduled Castes / Scheduled Tribes

"*Dalit Freedom - Now and Forever* is a graphic and compelling portrait of one of the epic struggles for the equality of man in the 21st century."

Luis Bush, Director, World Enquiry Coalition

Dedication:
This book is dedicated to two women: Agnes and Mariam. One taught me the meaning of integrity, truth and courage. The other sensitized me to the oppression of the Dalits and why it is critical to get involved in the struggle for justice.

In Memoriam:
This book is written in memory of Dr. B.R. Ambedkar and Mahatma Jotirao Phule, two great Indian leaders the world must get to know. They have been hidden for far too long.

The world knows about Mahatma Gandhi, but why is it that the world has not been told about this other Mahatma from India — Mahatma Phule?

DALIT Freedom

Now and Forever

The Epic Struggle for Dalit Emancipation

Joseph D'souza

Dalit Freedom Network

Dalit Freedom – Now And Forever
by Joseph D'souza

Copyright © 2004 by Joseph D'souza
First India Edition 2005

ISBN 0-9764290-0-4

Published by

Dalit Freedom Network
177 Presidency Ave.
Medchal Road., Jeedimetla Village
Secunderabad, Andhra Pradesh 500 055
INDIA

Email: info@dalitnetwork.org
Web: www.dalitnetwork.org

Designed, printed and bound by
OM Books, P.O.Box 2014, Secunderabad 500003
E-mail: publisher@omb.ind.om.org

Contents

Contents

Foreword:
A New Guide For New Action

Joseph D'souza is one of the world's great Christian leaders, fully sensitized to the Dalit plight in ideology, practice, and family, even though he comes from the upper caste sections of Indian Christians in Mangalore. He carries the great traditions of white Christians who raised the banner of revolt against slavery and racism in their nations. He is the President of the All India Christian Council (AICC) and its international counterpart in the USA, the Dalit Freedom Network. He is also the Associate International Director of OM International. He is one of the first major Christian leaders to globalize the issue of caste and to work for the abolition of caste and untouchability.

The AICC was born during a crisis of persecution and with the confidence of major and minor Christian denominations and churches in India. After coming to power in the Indian Government in 1996, the Hindutva organizations launched an attack on the Indian Church and all its denominations. The AICC was formed as an umbrella organization to protect the right of all Christian churches to propagate their religion and to ensure their human rights. In 2001, the AICC declared its support for the Dalit-Bahujan liberation struggles. The Hindutva organizations and the Bharatiya Janata Party (BJP) were historically strongly against spiritual equality for the Dalits, Tribals and Other Backward Castes (OBCs).

The priestly caste – the Brahmins – were against the lower castes gaining spiritual equality. Brahmins alone hold the most powerful position – temple priests – in their hands. They are also opposed to communicating with Hindu gods in any language other than Sanskrit. Historically, this language was not supposed to be learned by the Dalits, Tribals and OBCs. Because of this spiritual oppression, already four major regions of ancient India have gone into the fold of Islam – Afghanistan, Pakistan, Bangladesh and Kashmir. The violent clashes between Hinduism and Islam in the Indian sub-continent created conditions of conflict, including all forms of terrorism. Dr. D'souza realizes that the problem of Indian terrorism could be solved by abolishing caste in India.

Christian missionaries introduced the concept of a universal education and also English as a language that can be used in the Church, State and civil society. Since the dominant Christian churches were also in the hands of upper caste converts, they did not think of giving spiritual equality and an English education to the lower castes. The Hindutva leaders educated their children in English, but abused and attacked the Church when it started serving the Dalits, Tribals and OBCs. The AICC, under the leadership of Dr. D'souza, took a categorical stand in opposing caste practices within the Church, as well as in Hindu society. It challenged the Hindutva forces on all fronts. It openly declared that the right to choose one's religion is a universal human right. The Christian Church should openly welcome the Dalits, Tribals, OBCs and others if they choose to embrace Christianity. The world knows well that religion is not bound by territorial national boundaries. The people's nationalist right is to choose any faith they prefer. Hindu

Brahminism stagnated Indian society by forcefully keeping people inside the caste culture. Only spiritual democracy can move this stagnant society toward change. Without establishing spiritual democracy, even India's political democracy may evaporate in the near future.

Necessary professions like shepherding, tilling the soil to produce food, buffalo-, bull- and cow-rearing, tanning and making goods out of animal skin, making pots out of soft soils, and climbing trees to cut fruits to harness natural drinks were declared tasks of spiritual pollution in India. In a word, the dignity of labor was destroyed. By taking a clear stand on caste and the right to religion, Dr. D'souza has shown a new path for the world and for India.

He says repeatedly that the battle for Dalit-Bahujan rights to equality should be fought on all fronts, especially globally and particularly in America and Europe. The understanding of the Western world about caste and untouchability must change. India has been presented to them through the eyes of the Brahminical interpreters of the Indian reality. There is a deliberate silence on the issue of caste discrimination and atrocities in India. The magnitude of the atrocities continues to baffle Indian society. As a result, Dr. D'souza initiated a worldwide campaign against caste and untouchability. His efforts have started to change the mindset of the Western Church.

In the context of a post-Durban UN conference against caste and racial discrimination, the work done by Dr. D'souza and the committed team that works within organizations like the AICC, the Dalit Freedom Network and various other groups, has brought about a sea of change in the understanding of Western societies, states, media, and more particularly the Church. This small manifesto helps the world understand Dr.

D'souza's position on the question of religious freedom for Dalits, Tribals and OBCs, and also the role of the Church. It brings out the history of struggles endured by the oppressed masses of India and works out a program for liberation of the untouchable and oppressed communities in India. In the future, the campaigns of global human rights leaders, whether religious or secular, should focus on the abolition of untouchability and caste discrimination in India.

The world movement for socio-spiritual, political and economic equality becomes meaningless if caste and untouchability remain as they are in India. Dr. D'souza's efforts and clarion call for spiritual liberation of the Dalit-Bahujans of India gives a new hope for the oppressed and exploited masses of India and around the world.

Dr. Kancha Ilaiah
Professor of Political Science, Osmania University;
Author of Why I am Not a Hindu
October 17, 2004
Hyderabad, India

Dalit Hymn*
Words and Music by Joshua Moore and Randall Goodgame

Sing from the village, sing from the town
Sub Kooch Ho Sak-ee Dey
Sing everyone who has been cast down
Sub Kooch Ho Sak-ee Dey

Sweeping, weaving, tilling the earth
Sub Kooch Ho Sak-ee Dey
Show me the man to deny our worth
Sub Kooch Ho Sak-ee Dey

Skin of the buffalo declared unclean
Sub Kooch Ho Sak-ee Dey
Through revolution, we'll be redeemed
Sub Kooch Ho Sak-ee Dey

God made every man forward and free
Sub Kooch Ho Sak-ee Dey
Rich man, poor man, every man free
Sub Kooch Ho Sak-ee Dey

Emancipate, Emancipate, Prime Minister, Emancipate
Free the Dalit, Free the Dalit, Prime Minister, Free the Dalit
Heed Ambedkar, Heed Ambedkar, Prime Minister,
Heed Ambedkar
Caste is a lie, Caste is a lie, Prime Minister, Caste is a lie

Sub Kooch Ho Sak-ee Dey

**These lyrics are taken from a Punjabi-language hymn. "Sub Kooch Ho Sak-ee Dey"
can be translated "Anything is Possible with God".
www.caedmonscall.com*

Preface

The book *Dalit Freedom – Now and Forever,* by Joseph D'souza, reflects the socio-political saga of Indian society. Sincere readers will find it not merely the work of a journalist, a writer and a sociologist, but of an authentic person who is expressing his own experiences. The author is a devout Christian, but is different from many Christians in India because he has been able to diagnose accurately the disease that caste-based Hinduism has brought to India during 3,000 years of history.

Dalit liberation is the obvious passion of the author, which again distinguishes him from many other Christians. I can personally vouch for Dr. D'souza's passion for Dalit rights, beginning with the great historical events of November 4, 2001, in Delhi, when far more than 100,000 Dalits exited Hinduism. Joseph D'souza, being President of the All Indian Christian Council and President of OM India, did not waver an inch from his stance of solidarity with the Dalits, despite Hindutva wrath. It is simple to write about a subject; but it is much more difficult to become an activist first, and then become an author. D'souza is a unique combination of both.

When Mrs. Sonia Gandhi joined Indian politics, the directionless Congress party sprang to life. The Bharatiya Janata Party and the RSS recognized her as a political threat and started attacking Christians. This suited their overall strategy of

19

targeting the Christians. As a consequence, whatever small scope for religious freedom remained within the nation was violently curtailed during the attacks on churches and the killing of Graham Staines. Terror reigned everywhere, Christians were frightened to preach the Gospel openly, and a few Christians were even forced to stop doing Christian work altogether.

At that time, Dr. D'souza understood the limitations Christians faced in fighting the Hindutva forces. However, he declared his support for the All India Confederation of Dalit Organizations and the Dalit International Foundation. Christians were thereby allied with the Dalits. He extended this cooperation and solidarity with Dalits across India. But then, as always, the Hindutva forces turned their attention to the Dalits. They completely closed the door for Dalit conversion by enacting illegal laws in obvious opposition to accepted human rights. These were the so-called "freedom of religion" bills which were, in actuality, anti-conversion laws. However, the combined campaign of Christians, Dalits, Bahujans and other minorities kept religious freedom alive in India, even though the Hindutva forces are constantly working against it. It is clear that Dr. D'souza's efforts, in conjunction with the alliances formed with the Dalits, have made quite an impact.

In this book, the author has honestly considered caste discrimination within the Indian Church, in addition to exposing the Hindutva agenda. It is revealing to me that the life and message of Christ influences America so strongly, even though North Americans have had the Gospel only since the 17th and 18th centuries. Somehow, despite the fact that the Apostle Thomas visited India in the first century A.D., the majority of villages and towns within India are still devoid of Christ.

Similarly, in my observation, Christians originating from an upper caste background socialize mainly along caste lines.

Dalit Christians, however, are marginalized. They have little influence in churches, Christian mission organizations, Christian-run health care facilities, and Christian-run educational institutions. It seems the Indian Church actively discriminates against its own. These compelling points prove to me the contention that caste discrimination within the Church has greatly hindered the spread of the Gospel in India.

D'souza also addresses the issue of globalization. Economic globalization has affected nearly everyone on earth. The upper castes in India welcome economic globalization (i.e., foreign investment, technology, and international brands), but avoid a globalization of faith, worldview, ideology and related subjects. D'souza, being a true patriot, is genuinely concerned about economic gains for the nation of India. However, for economic betterment to transpire, cultural globalization must come first, working to relieve the oppression caused by 3,000 years of caste. Unfortunately, Indian industries oppose affirmative action in the private sector, unlike Western countries. Globalization of culture means adopting those parts of the First-world worldview which have helped Western nations progress (i.e., guaranteed human rights, equality of all human beings, dignity of labor, equal opportunity, affirmative action for the disenfranchised, freedom of speech, and genuine freedom of religion and conscience). It does not mean completely forsaking the rich heritage and culture of India's majority people.

The Western press, missionaries, business houses, non-profit organizations, and governments have also failed in good measure to discharge their duties, especially in the present age of globalization. Most of the time, Western interest is purely economic. Even though they talk about overall progress and development, this is not on their primary agenda.

This book is a call for the USA and other Western nations to insist on true progress, development and growth. This will mean a global movement that works to end the caste discrimination and oppression that exists in different levels of society in India and around the world. The West must be willing to let the best parts of all global cultures flow without restriction. The Dalits of India must find full socio-spiritual emancipation and empowerment in this generation.

Dalits are in utmost despair because of economic globalization. The benefits go nearly completely to the elitist upper castes. In addition, whatever jobs exist in the private sector remain unreachable for the Dalits because of their lack of quality English-medium education.

Mahatma Phule aptly noted that the British collapsed under the pressure of Brahminical forces and removed the teachings of Christ from the Indian educational system during their Raj. In the new millennium, why can't Westerners question why there is the free flow of teachings on Hinduism in their part of the world, while at the same time the Dalits and the Backward Castes in India do not have the same freedom to learn about other religious ideologies? Why is the West so silent when religious freedom is taken from the Dalits? I experienced this brute use of the State's power in 2001.

Further, very disturbingly, even the charity of Western countries, including the USA, is not ultimately reaching the Dalits. It is instead being swallowed up by the so-called affluent castes. The time has come to discover exactly where Western charity is going.

The Western media has been relatively unable to capture the caste reality and discrimination of India. It is only now that a few news agencies have realized that they have missed the tyrannical injustice based on birth that caste has inflicted on the nation of India.

I hope that this book will help them in understanding the phenomenon better. The West must wake up to the fact that caste continues to dominate and oppress the Indian nation.

This book contains some of the writings of Dr. B.R. Ambedkar who exhorted Dalits to quit Hinduism. He opined that Hinduism was not a religion, but was instead a political scheme crafted by the microscopic upper castes to rule the rest of the nation. It would be in the interest of the supporters of Hindutva to reform their religion by allowing a healthy competitiveness among various religions.

The appendix written by Dr. Kancha Ilaiah, "Cow and Culture", substantiates the miseries of Dalits who are deemed less important than cows, dogs, snakes and other wild animals. The so-called upper castes can touch these animals and worship them, but they still consider physical contact with Dalits polluting.

In Christian ideology, God gave all power to the Ultimate Victim; but in Hinduism, those D'souza calls the "supreme victims" – the Dalits of history – remain "supreme victims". The story is told of how a great Dalit saint, Sambuk, was killed by Lord Ram because he dared to worship Hindu gods. Dalits have no access to God and what Sambuk did was therefore offensive to the upper castes. Today the situation is no different. Neither Sambuk nor his Dalit people have ever found redemption or power.

I know the busy schedule of the author, and appreciate the time he took to pen this important book. His authorship is commendable and will certainly be helpful in the cause of Dalit freedom, liberation and salvation.

Dr. Udit Raj
President, Justice Party; Chairman, All India Confederation of
Scheduled Castes / Scheduled Tribes
October 22, 2004, New Delhi

Introduction

This small book would never have been written if not for the rise of the Hindutva ideology and its proponents' incessant attacks against Christians. Hate literature, false propaganda and physical attacks on Christian workers and churches, and the harassment of the State forced us to ask: Why did the Hindu extremists target Indian Christians? Why this hate culture and why the burning of Graham Staines and his sons?

Christians lived as peaceful citizens in the country and were not involved in any communal clashes or violent activities. Our neighbors loved us and we continue to be as patriotic and nationalistic as any other Indian.

As a Christian leader with over 25 years experience in all kinds of compassionate Christian work across the nation, and as someone who has networked with all branches of Christianity in India and in other parts of the world, I knew of no evidence of the false propaganda accusing Christians of engaging in forced and fraudulent conversions. If anything, Christian workers were quietly carrying on their faithful compassionate activities and witness to Christ.

As a quiet, confident Indian Christian leader who stands up for the independence and autonomy of the Indian Church in global Christian forums, it was strange for me to experience the insinuation that we were tools in the hands of some foreign powers.

Like my compatriots, I love being an Indian. I love India, its culture and its way of life. India is a great nation. I love our vast and diverse heritage. I admire the nation building process that has been going on since Independence in which Indian Christians, along with others, have played a major role.

Yet there has been a systematic campaign of hate and attack hatched against us by the Sangh Parivar. As we researched the persecution against Christians, it became apparent that it was not primarily about us. It was about the Dalits. It was about the Bahujans. India has been in major caste turmoil for the last couple of decades. This upheaval has changed the social and political landscape of the nation.

There is no question about it. Many of the Dalits want out of the heinous caste system. Politicians have not delivered. Dalit atrocities are mounting by the day. In many places, the State is a mute spectator. What is written in the Constitution does not work itself out in the villages and towns of India where Dalit women are raped, abused, tortured, paraded naked and humiliated. In the previous BJP President's village in Andhra Pradesh, Dalits cannot drink water from the same well as the upper castes.

Thus began many meetings and discussions with Dalit-Bahujan leaders. These meetings took place all across the nation and we Christians were immersed immediately into the Dalit-Bahujan struggle. Our mentors and teachers were now Dalit-Bahujan leaders and intellectuals. They were not Christians. We listened to them. We repented before them for caste discrimination within the Indian Church. Dalit-Bahujan leaders continue to talk to us and advise us.

We began to see why Christians are one of the greatest threats to the Hindutva brigade: we will welcome the Dalits into the body of Christ. That is the nature of Christ's teaching. If Dalits choose freely to turn to our faith, we will not reject them. If they want help, we will not turn them away. The Dalits and the OBCs have lost out spiritually, socially and developmentally in the last 50 years, not to mention what has happened to them in the past 3,500 years. A tiny minority continues to enjoy the riches, wealth and privileges of India. This minority rules and manages the richest temples of India and controls the nation's temple economy which is one of the economic power centers of Indian society.

The Brahminical caste ideology helps them maintain their socio-spiritual monopoly. The casteist Hindutva movement is aimed at duping the Dalit-Bahujan people further. Dalit-Bahujan recruits are used to kill Christians, Muslims and others who do not subscribe to the Hindutva agenda. Christians and Muslims are portrayed as "enemies."

Hindutva subscribers in the West who enjoy the wealth and fruit of Western democracies send money to finance the Sangh Parivar and to keep Brahminism alive.

We realized that if we stayed silent, we would be silenced forever. We realized that we had to join the Dalit-Bahujan struggle for socio-spiritual freedom and liberation by using all non-violent means to fight those responsible for the oppression of the vast majority of Indians. This is why Christians are the greatest threat to Hindutva.

The struggle is far from over. Only when the Dalit-Bahujan peoples become socio-spiritually free, live with equal dignity, and are masters of their own fate and destiny in their own nation, will the struggle be over.

This book is just a small introduction to this complex phenomenon that besets my great nation.

The chapters in the Appendix section have been carefully chosen because they shed light on important facets of the struggle for Dalit emancipation. I encourage you to read them as they will provide additional background and insight.

There are many who have made this book possible and I want to express my thanks to all of them. I especially owe a lot of gratitude to Dalit-Bahujan intellectuals and leaders who have instructed me. My deepest gratitude also goes to the progressive upper caste leaders, especially the women, who encouraged me to take a proactive stand on this issue and not be intimidated by the Hindutva forces. A special thanks also to my assistant, K. Lajja, who helped in drafting this manuscript.

May the Dalits achieve Freedom – Now and Forever.

Joseph D'souza
Hyderabad, India
October 20, 2004

Notes on Terms and Concepts

Ambedkar, Dr. B.R.: Hailing from central India in the early 1900s, Ambedkar is known as the champion of the Dalits. Dr. Ambedkar was born into one of the lowest sectors of the Dalit caste hierarchy. Overcoming the many educational obstacles facing Dalits, he received his M.A., Ph.D., D.Sc., and L.L.D. in Law from Colombia University, USA, and London. Additionally, he received a D.Lit. from Osmania University in Hyderabad, India. He is known as the Father of the Indian Constitution. The Dalit movement for socio-spiritual freedom began with him. He was driven from one school to another, was forced to take classes outside the classroom, and was thrown out of hotels in the dead of night because he was considered untouchable.

Aryans: The word 'Aryan' means 'royal' or 'noble'. The Aryan people are fair in complexion. When they arrived in India more than 3,000 years ago, they considered themselves racially superior to all others, including the original inhabitants of India (the Dravidians and the aboriginals). They were responsible for the present caste system and the practice of untouchability in India.

Bahujan: Bahujans are considered the oppressed communities within the caste system. They are known as the low or backward

29

castes, and though theoretically higher in socio-spiritual status than the Dalits, they do not enjoy equal rights or privileges with the upper castes.

Brahma: Brahma is one of the members of the chief Hindu godhead which consists of three main gods (the other two being Vishnu and Shiva). While millions of other gods are worshiped within Hinduism, these three compose the main triumvirate in the Hindu scriptures and are generally considered most powerful and important. Brahma was the first god and Hindus consider him the God of gods.

Brahmin: Not to be confused with Brahma (one of the gods of Hinduism). The Brahmin people are the priestly class, the highest of the four divisions in ancient Hindu society. Strictly speaking, a Brahmin is one who knows and repeats the Vedas (Hindu scriptures). Brahmins conduct all the ritual affairs of Hindu society.

Buddhism: A religion founded by Gautama Buddha who was from a ruling caste (Kshatriya). He vehemently fought against Brahminical domination in the religious sphere and caste injustice in society.

Caste: According to Hinduism, people are innately divided into four groups called castes or varnas. The groups are Brahmin (the priestly caste); Kshatriya (the warrior caste and protectors of Hinduism); Vaishya (the business community); and Sudra (the supportive workers serving the three upper castes). Considered unclean and even lower in status than animals, the Dalits do not belong to this pyramid of castes and are therefore known as outcastes. The Brahmins comprise less than five percent of the total population, but they have maintained domination of Indian power, politics and religion for thousands of years. This was true even during the British Raj.

Christianity: Christianity is a religion that has a spiritual democratic tradition and culture. Jesus is the source of its faith, culture and traditions.

Dalit: The root for the word 'Dalit' is found both in Hebrew and in Sanskrit. It refers to people who are socially, religiously, economically and politically oppressed, deprived and exploited in India. The word 'Dalit' is often used to describe a person who comes from any lower caste, even though technically authentic Dalits are kept outside the caste system as unworthy to enter the social and religious life of society. They are generally considered to be polluted socially, poor economically and powerless politically. They are not allowed to touch caste Hindus and are therefore treated as 'untouchables'. Dalits are found spread throughout the nation of India, South Asia and among the Indian diaspora around the world.

Dravidians: Dravidians are the original inhabitants of India, mainly dark in complexion. They lived in the northern part of India and were pushed southward by the Aryan invaders.

Fascism: A school of thought that established oppressive conditions all over the world.

Hindu: The word 'Hindu' is derived from the Sanskrit word 'Sindhu' (a river – more specifically, the Indus). The Persians in the fifth century BC called the Hindus by that name, identifying them as the people of the land of the Indus. The religion of the

Hindu people was therefore known as Hinduism. The term Hindu was coined by medieval Muslim scholars.

Hindutva: The philosophy of right-wing fundamentalist Hinduism. It believes that India is for Hindus and should be ruled only by Hindus. The Hindutva forces believe in inseparability of politics and religion. Minorities should abide by and live at the mercy or goodwill of the majority. The Hindutva regime would like to establish one race (Hindu), one culture (Hindu) and one religion (Hinduism) in the Indian sub-continent. All other religious groups are considered a minority. Hindutva ideology is dominated by Brahminism.

Kshatriya: This is the second most powerful caste in India. It is the ruling caste. Their welfare depends upon their respect for the priestly caste (Brahmins).

Mulnivasi: The original inhabitants of India. This term is used to include Dalits, Backwards, Other Backwards, and those converted to Christianity, Islam or Buddhism in different phases of Indian history.

RSS: Rastriya Swam Sevak Sangh. This is a Hindu extremist organization with a wide Hindu network. They have appointed themselves the guardians of India and the Hindu religion. They vehemently oppose Christianity and other minority religions in India. They are responsible for the false propaganda and hate campaign against minorities in India. They believe in violence as a divine necessity. Therefore, they distribute weapons openly and freely.

Scheduled Castes (SC): The Scheduled Castes are the people who come from the lowest of the Hindu castes. They are non-tribal by heritage. Government records use this term to refer to the Dalits, even though technically Dalits are in reality kept outside the caste system.

Scheduled Tribes (ST): Scheduled Tribes are the aboriginals of India. They, too, are oppressed and exploited by the higher castes and are kept outside the caste system. Earlier they were considered the criminal tribes by the upper castes. Most of these people live in the mountain regions and forest zones of India. The Scheduled Castes and Scheduled Tribes often come together to stand up for their rights, even though they are different by family heritage.

Sanskrit: Sanskrit is the historical language of the Hindu religion. It is the language of the elite and high caste Brahmins. Most of the Hindu scriptures were written in Sanskrit. The language is generally learned only by the priestly caste. According to Manu, the law giver, Dalits should not even hear the reading of the scripture in Sanskrit. If this happens, boiled lead should be poured into the offending Dalit's ears.

Tribal: Tribals are the original people of India. Today they are forced to live in the jungles. They are exploited by the three upper castes.

Vaishya: Vaishyas are third in the order of the upper caste hierarchy. They are responsible for business within Hindu society. Mahatma Gandhi belonged to this caste.

VHP: Vishwa Hindu Parishad. This is one of the many Hindu extremist organizations within India and around the world. They are registered in the USA as a 501(c)3 organization. In India they are notorious for their hate campaigns against Christians, and for inciting communal violence. Money that is raised in the West is sent out to further their agenda in India. They have led the attacks on minorities such as Christians and Muslims in India. They are largely responsible for the false propaganda and hate campaign against the minorities in India. They are the ones who conducted mass murders in Gujarat and subsequently tried to justify their actions.

Untouchables: (Dalits) Untouchables are considered so unworthy by the upper caste echelon that they are not part of the caste system. Untouchables are forbidden from physically touching any member of any caste. Doing so would render the latter "unclean" by Hindu scriptural law. Thus, the Dalits are commonly known as "untouchables". Other varieties of untouchability include "unseeables" (those who cannot be seen by a caste person) and "unapproachables" (those who cannot come near to a caste person).

Chapter One
Killed for Skinning a Dead Cow

It is a story too cruel to imagine – too inhuman – yet shockingly true. Five Dalits were brutally lynched in Jhajjar, Haryana, on October 15, 2002. What was their crime? Skinning a dead cow and transporting the cowhide. Was this illegal? Was it an offense to society? Absolutely not. In fact, the skinning of cows and the transporting of cowhide is a traditional occupation for a sizeable number of Dalits. It is an occupation assigned to them by the caste into which they were born. These five Dalits were mercilessly murdered simply for fulfilling their role in a caste-based society. However, the casteist forces believed their murderous act to be righteous. They killed these five Dalits because they believed the Dalits had first killed the cow, a holy animal, before skinning it.

Indian civil society was outraged. The cries of injustice heard around the nation were spontaneous and widespread. Progressive Hindus across the nation also raised their voices. In contrast, soon after the incident, Giriraj Kishore, the Vice President of the Vishwa Hindu Parishad (VHP, a fundamentalist organization promoting Hindutva values across India), celebrated the killing of these five Dalits. He proclaimed the life of a cow more valuable than the life of a human being (read Dalit). Another Hindu religious leader said that people must learn to live in the caste into which they were born. The local government's response was lethargic. Once again, the caste monster had reared its ugly head.

The Dalits of the state of Haryana were shocked, angered and agitated. Moreover, they felt saddened because they knew this was not an isolated event.

Human Rights Watch reports, "Between 1994 and 1996, a total of 98,349 cases were registered with the police nationwide as crimes and atrocities against Schedule Castes. Of these, 38,483 were registered under the 1989 Scheduled Castes/Tribes Atrocities Act. A further 1,160 were for murder, 2,814 for rape, and 13,671 for hurt. Given that Dalits are both reluctant and unable (for lack of police cooperation) to report crimes against themselves, the actual number of abuses is presumably much higher."[1] These statistics are ten years old. At this rate, 153

Dalit children are the youngest victims of caste discrimination

Caste-based oppression subjects Dalits to extreme poverty

Dalits are being physically tortured every day; six every hour. Today the atrocities are rising in frequency and in intensity by the minute.

The Indian Government made efforts to control atrocities against the Dalits. Though the Constitution of India bans untouchability,[2] it does not outlaw the caste system. Though it bans discrimination based on caste, it has not eliminated the caste 'virus' in Indian society. The caste system is so deeply ingrained in the Indian cultural worldview through thousands of years of reinforcement that these attempts at granting equality have been largely ineffective.

The Indian Government also offers economic assistance to Dalits. In an effort to ease their plight, the Constitution instituted and guaranteed an economic/social system called "Compensatory Discrimination" or "Reservation". This system grants some privileges to the Dalits through reservations (affirmative action) in government-run schools, colleges and institutions. A percentage of government jobs and parliamentary[3] positions are reserved for the Dalit people.

These concessions, though, face difficulty in application. Why? A combination of the Indian social worldview, a lack of English-medium educated Dalits, and a caste-based bias by those filling positions available through affirmative action prevents the success of the reservation system.

While in theory this welfare measure extended to the Dalits should help eliminate discrimination, in reality the Dalits continue to endure centuries-long oppression, struggling for their human rights. Society simply refuses to relinquish caste. Since its inception thousands of years ago, it has been the dominant force binding India together into an oppressive culture and social system.

Notes:
1. Human Rights Watch, <u>Broken People</u>, Bangalore, 1999, p. 41.
2. Article 17 abolishes "Untouchability". Its practice in any form is an offense punishable under law. No article in the Constitution was adopted with such unanimity and so great an acclamation and enthusiasm as this article. To enforce this law, in 1955 "The Untouchability Offenses Act" came into force. The 1955 Act was amended in 1976 and came to be known as "The Protection of Civil Rights Act". One significant new provision of the Act is that a person convicted of an untouchability offense will be disqualified from running for public office.
3. Under article 330, 114 seats are reserved in the Parliament and 691 seats are reserved in the state assemblies.

Chapter Two
Caste and its Consequences for the Dalits

According to widely accepted theory, Hinduism started as an amalgamation of three different religious traditions – Aryanism (the religion of the Aryans who worshiped Vishnu and came to India during the second millennium before Christ), Dravidianism (the religion of the Dravidians who worshiped Shiva), and Animism (the religion of the tribal people[4] who worshiped nature).

When the Aryans invaded India more than 3,500 years ago, they fought and subdued the native Dravidians and other original inhabitants. To maintain their purity of race, the Aryan invaders created their own social order and divided the community. This was the beginning of the caste system and the inception of social and economic segregation ordered and organized by the Aryan invaders. As time passed, this social order, which became known as the caste system, gained Hindu religious sanction.

The *Manusmriti* book of Hindu holy legal code outlined the social order governing Hindu society. This society was divided into four castes.[5] Each caste, as theologically explained by the Vedas (the Hindu scriptures), allegedly descended from a specific part of the body of the Hindu god, Brahma. The three upper castes (Brahmins, Kshatriyas, Vaishyas) made up 15 percent of the population and were taken from the head, the arms/shoulder and the belly/thigh of Brahma, respectively.

Still today, the highest caste, the Brahmins, make up approximately four percent of the total population of India. This minority, however, holds most of the power in the nation. They have ruled the Indian population for thousands of years. The Sudras, or the Slave castes (today called the Backward Castes and comprising 50-52 percent of the population), were said to have come from Brahma's feet. Of the total population, an estimated 16-25 percent are untouchables who do not belong to any of the four castes. The Aryans deemed their professions (i.e., tanning of leather, sweeping the streets, or cleaning and carrying human excrement) unclean. The people became the outcastes and the so-called "criminal tribes", a terminology used to position the tribals of India. The aboriginal tribals constitute about eight percent of the population. The remaining members of society belong to the minority religions like Islam, Christianity, Sikhism and Buddhism.

While the Vedas set forth the theological basis for the caste system, it was Manu, the Hindu law giver, who codified the strict caste rules rationalizing the oppression of Dalits today. Manu's rules reduced the Dalits to be worth less than animals, making them the object of abuse, exploitation and oppression.[6] These caste rules bound the Dalits to degrading manual labor under the regime of the upper castes. Dalits accepted their fate, believing they had done unspeakable acts in previous lives, that God did not love them, that they were born to serve the upper castes, and that they had no rights. Manu's rules implemented these alleged divine tenets on a practical level. Temple entry, for instance, was prohibited for the Dalits and Sudras. (The lower castes were allotted their own gods, goddesses and festivals.) They could not come in contact with those within the caste system. Even stray dogs could enter freely into the presence of upper caste men and women, but the Dalits could not. Though scripted thousands of years ago, these tragic conditions continue to exist, even today, for India's Dalits.

Mahatma Gandhi, in an effort to rectify the situation, called Dalits 'Harijans' meaning 'the children of God'. However, Gandhi's unwillingness to tackle the whole issue of the caste system rather than merely its symptoms has led the Dalits to distance themselves from the term Harijans which today is seen as derogatory. Dr. John Dayal of the All India Christian Council gives reference to the origin of the word 'Harijan': "The term Harijan means literally, people of Hari, one of the Hindu trinity. In common use it means children of God. Originally it was used by one Narsi Mehta of Gujarat for the Dalit people. It was census

The word "Harijans" originally referred to children born to temple prostitutes

Dalits are forced to do work the upper castes consider unclean

time during the British regime. They wanted to give communal representation to the Dalits. However, the census officers faced a problem. There were many thousands of Dalit children who did not know the name of their fathers. These children were born of mothers forced into temple prostitution. The dominant caste men would use such 'dedicated' Dalit women for sex inside and in the vicinity of the temples. Disparagingly, Narsi Mehta said it would be appropriate to call such Dalit children 'children of Hari' as they were born of sex that took place in the name of gods."[7]

The untouchables themselves have adopted the term 'Dalit' referring to a status or condition, not to caste position. 'Dalit'[8] is derived from a Sanskrit equivalent meaning 'crushed', 'broken', or 'downtrodden', accurately reflecting the Dalits' desperate condition as they endure social, religious, economic and political oppression.[9]

India's Dalits number approximately 250 million men, women and children. Still today, Dalits are deemed low and backward in the social structure and are denied even basic human rights. They are commonly refused entry to public parks and temples. Use of public wells is denied, and many restaurants keep separate drinking glasses or clay cups for Dalit use. Their women are frequently abused and sold into prostitution. Finding a place to bury their dead is a problem. Seventy percent of Dalits live below the poverty line. Only two to three percent of Dalit women can read and write. Millions of Dalit children serve as bonded laborers.

Dalit women face unimaginable atrocities

The book *Broken People: Caste Violence Against India's Untouchables*, a report by Smita Narula, researcher for the Asian Division of Human Rights Watch, catalogues some of the worst examples of the mistreatment of Dalits as they are stripped of the most basic human rights. Following is just a small sampling of stories from this candid book which reflects accurately both past and present examples of Dalit persecution.

Guruammal

"I am a 26-year-old Dalit agricultural laborer. I earn 20 rupees per day (US $0.44) for a full day's work. In December 1997, the police raided my village . . . The superintendent of police [SP] called me a pallachi, which is a caste name for prostitute. He then opened his pants [zipper] . . . At 11:00 a.m., the sub-collector came. I told the collector that the SP had opened his [zipper] and used a vulgar word. I also told him that they had broken my silver pot. The SP was angry I had pointed him out . . .

"The next morning the police broke all the doors and arrested all the men in the village . . . The SP came looking for me. My husband hid under the [bed]. My mother was with me at the time. I was in my night clothes. The police started calling me a prostitute and started beating me. The SP dragged me naked on the road for 100 feet. I was four months pregnant at the time . . . A 60-year-old woman asked them to stop. They beat her, too, and fractured her hands . . . They brought me to the police station naked . . . 53 men had been arrested. One of them took off his lungi [wrap-around cloth] and gave it to me to cover myself.

"I begged the police officers at the jail to help me. I even told them I was pregnant. They mocked me for making such bold statements to the police the day before. I spent 25 days in

Many young Dalit girls are forced to work long hours for little pay

jail. I miscarried my baby after 10 days. Nothing has happened to the officers who did this to me."[10]

Massacre at Shankarbigha

"On the evening of January 25, 1999, at least 22 Dalit men, women and children were killed in the village of Shankarbigha . . . The massacre was the fifth of its kind since July 1996 in which Dalit and lower-caste men, women and children were killed . . . According to press reports, [the perpetrators] entered eight thatched huts in the village during the night and fired indiscriminately on the occupants. Many of

Dalit women are deemed worthless in caste-based society

the victims, including several children, were shot in the head and stomach at point-blank range . . . The police ignored early warnings that a massacre was likely . . . Twenty-four people were arrested in late January 1999 in connection to the massacre . . . Activists are pessimistic, however, that any will be prosecuted."[11]

Andhrachak

"Some 300 police officers surrounded 50 homes and arrested six [Dalit] people. Ranjeet, a 38-year-old Dalit agricultural laborer, witnessed the arrest of his brother, father and cousin. 'The first time they came at 4:30 p.m., they didn't take anyone. They came into all the houses. They took my friend's torches, his tobacco box and 500 rupees out of the money box. They ransacked all the rooms and broke the pots and doors. We ran because we were afraid of being beaten . . . They also beat my brother's wife with the butt of their gun. They hit her on her backside; she had to seek treatment. The second time they came it was 4:00 a.m. The people they arrested were also beaten with sticks . . . I went to jail to get them released. They said they would only give bail after [national parliamentary] elections. They said it is 1,000 rupees (US $22) for bail. We will have to get a loan.'"[12]

The Ramabai Killings

"On July 11, 1997, residents of Ramabai Ambedkar Nagar, a predominantly Dalit-populated colony in Bombay, woke to find their statue of Dr. Ambedkar desecrated by a garland of sandals around his neck. The placing of shoes or sandals around the neck of the likeness of a person is taken as a sign of extreme disrespect and is usually an attempt to denigrate that person and his or her beliefs. When residents complained of the desecration . . . they were told to lodge a complaint at the . . . police station. By 7:00 a.m. the growing crowd began protesting . . . Within minutes, members of the Special Reserve Police Force (SRPF) . . . arrived in a van . . . hundreds of meters away from the statue and the protesters on the highway. SRPF constables opened fire on pedestrians on the service road in front of the colony and later into alleys between colony houses. The firing lasted for ten to fifteen minutes and killed ten people. Most of the victims were shot above the waist. Five hours later, at 11:30 a.m., at a site 150 meters away from the firing and 300 meters away from the desecrated statue, an angry crowd set fire to a luxury bus. At 2:00 p.m., 20-25 police officers entered Ramabai colony, started spreading tear gas, and began lathi-charging residents in their homes. At 4:00 p.m. they lathi-charged again. By late afternoon, 26 people had been seriously injured."[13]

Sold into Prostitution

"Thousands of untouchable female children (between six and eight years old) are forced to become maidens of God (Devadasis, Jogins, a Hindu religious practice in Andhra Pradesh, Karnataka, Maharashtra, and Orissa, to mention only a few). They are taken from their families, never to see them again. They are later raped by the temple priest and finally auctioned secretly into prostitution and ultimately die from AIDS. It is estimated by NGOs that 5,000 to 15,000 girls are auctioned secretly every year."[14]

Women: The Bottom of Society

"Dalit women are at the bottom in our community. Within the women's movement, Dalit issues have not been taken seriously. Within the Dalit movement, women have been ignored. Caste, class, and gender need to be looked at together . . . Women's labor is already undervalued; when she is a Dalit, it is nil . . . The atrocities are also much more vulgar. Making women eat human defecation, parading them naked, gang rapes, these are women-specific crimes. Gang rapes are mostly of Dalit women. These cases should be given top priority, requiring immediate action and immediate punishment."[15]

Today's situation for the Dalit people is no different from the above examples from the 1990s. Khalid Azam tells of a place in Tamil Nadu where Dalits in a village "are forced to walk barefoot, eat in coconut shells and even bow... to their landlords . . . These people have been facing discrimination for ages with each generation inheriting the derogatory customs and rules . . . in their most primitive form. The Dalits live in separate colonies and are forbidden from entering restaurants, shops and even kiosks. At tea stalls they are made to sit in special enclosures and served in either coconut shells or disposable plastic cups instead of the usual steel tumblers used for others."[16]

Shockingly, the discrimination and oppression of the Dalits is not limited to India. Dalits in other parts of the world also face these atrocities. Tom Brake, MP, Liberal Democrat

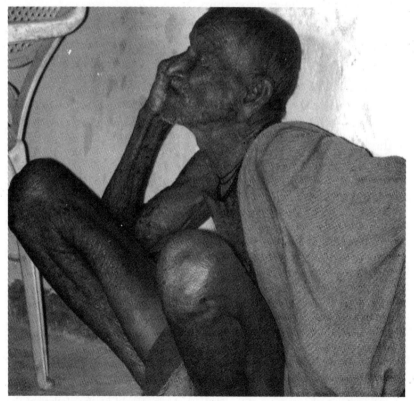

Finding food, clothing and shelter is a problem for the Dalits

Member of Parliament for Carshalton and Wallington, and Shadow Secretary of State for International Development (England), said in a recent parliamentary debate, "Even in the UK there is discrimination against the Dalits. I met some Dalits recently, one of whom is a senior person working at a hospital in Ealing. He said that not he but a woman Dalit colleague of his had encountered enormous problems in establishing her authority as a manager, because the people of a higher caste with whom she worked did not recognize that she could possibly manage them. He said that there was even graffiti in the hospital. Simply the word 'caste', to remind her that she had no authority in the caste system."[17]

As these disturbing examples plainly indicate, casteism is worse than racism. The oppressor turns into an inhuman monster. The oppressed become sub-human creatures emptied of their humanity and dignity. The caste plot of Indian civilization is a tragedy unlike anything else. Caste dehumanizes both the oppressors – the elitist upper castes – and the oppressed – the low castes.

Notes:
4. The tribal people are called Adivasis, which means "the original inhabitants". The Hindu fundamentalist forces did not like this term because it implied that all others were intruders or invaders. Therefore, they preferred the term "Vanavasis" or "jungle people" because most of them lived in the jungles and were chased by the invading Aryans who seized the land of the original inhabitants.
5. Priests (Brahmins), rulers or warrior kings (Kshatriyas), the common people (Vaishyas), and servants (Sudras). Their creation from the mouth and other parts of the primordial man is described in Rg Veda 10.90. For details of The Law of Manu please refer: Wendy Doniger and Brian K. Smith, The Law of Manu, New Delhi, 1991.
6. Manu prescribed that they should live near mounds, trees, cremation grounds, in mountains and in groves, recognizable and making a living by their own innate activities. They should live outside the village, and dogs and donkeys should be their wealth. Their clothing should be the clothes of the

dead, and their food should be in broken dishes; their ornaments should be made of black iron, and they should wander constantly.

7. Personal email correspondence from John Dayal, October 18, 2004.

8. According to James Massey, "Historically, the roots of the term Dalit go back even to the pre-Biblical Hebrew and pre-classical Sanskrit era. Its ancient form is found in the east Semitic group of languages, especially known as Akkadian. The present usage of the term Dalit goes back to the nineteenth century, when a Marathi social reformer and revolutionary, Mahatma Jotirao Phule, used it to describe the outcastes and untouchables as the oppressed and broken victims of our caste-ridden society. Massey 1994, 6.

9. The word Dalit could also mean the torn, the rent, the burst, the split, the opened, the expanded, the bisected, the driven asunder, the dispelled, the scattered, the downtrodden, the crushed, the destroyed, the manifested or the displayed.

10. Broken People, p. i.

11. Ibid., pp. 58-59.

12. Ibid., p. 77.

13. Ibid., pp. 127-8.

14. Ibid., p. 151.

15. Ibid., pp. 166-7.

16. Khalid Azam, "India Thinkers Net" Yahoo! Groups internet discussion group, June 29, 2004.

17. Tom Brake MP, excerpt from transcript of debate in Hansard, England, on the topic of slavery. See www.parliament.the-stationery-office.co.uk.

Chapter Three
The Most Valuable Freedom

One of the key issues caste-based oppression brings to the forefront of human thought and debate is freedom of conscience. Dalit oppression is a nightmare in and of itself. Additionally, however, Dalits are denied a fundamental human right: the freedom of conscience, which is the ability to make individual choices, especially with regard to religious beliefs and moral activity. The denial of this right completes the Dalit hell on earth.

Dalits are permanently bonded to their status as outcastes. There is nothing within Indian society that can make them upper castes – not even education, money or position, as Dr. B.R. Ambedkar and others discovered to their deep sadness. The upper castes' demand for full subservience by the Dalits has only intensified under the growth of the extremist Hindutva movement. Tens of thousands of copies of the much despised book by Manu detailing the caste system have been distributed in the villages and towns of India in recent years. The growth of the Hindutva movement coincided with a directly proportional increase in the number of atrocities against Dalits. Every attempt is made to maintain the power structure of the upper castes. Without the slavery of the caste system, the

Without freedom of conscience, Dalits are imprisoned in their oppression

whole edifice of the upper caste power structure comes apart religiously, socially and economically.

Early in modern India's history, a Presidential ordinance allegedly created "protection" for the Dalits. However, in actuality, the State became party to wider discrimination against the Dalits. The State decided to favor those who had the label "Hindu" even though the Dalits have had no rights within the Hindu caste system for over 3,000 years. The ordinance initially favored the granting of affirmative action privileges only to those Dalits labeled Hindu. Dalits of other faiths had no access to these privileges. Once again the Dalits were obviously targeted.

Paradoxically, force and allurement has been used to retain the Dalit people in a system that forever considers them outcastes. Concurrently, there is no law giving Dalits full and free rights within the Hindu caste system. Dalits cannot become priests in a temple. Dalits cannot become the high priests of the Hindu religion and occupy the status of a Shankaracharya (the main acknowledged seats or thrones of Hinduism).

Because of this systematic discrimination on the religious front and in the realm of the conscience, the silent exodus of the Dalits from the Brahminical social order continues unabated. It is critical to understand that this is an exodus of revolt against an evil and sinful structure. Those who are "sinned against" are freely and willingly striking back at their oppressors spiritually and socially. There is neither force nor fraudulent means being employed by Christians or by any of the other faiths the Dalits are currently embracing.

The movement by Dalits to other religions continues in events such as the conversions to Islam at Meenakshipuram, Tamil Nadu, nearly 20 years ago; the conversion of an estimated 100,000 Dalits on November 4, 2001, to Buddhism in New Delhi; and the conversion of Dalits to Buddhism and Christianity in Chennai and Bangalore in the last couple of years.

With regard to the conversions to Islam over 20 years ago at Meenakshipuram, a recent news magazine survey reported that there was not a single Dalit out of the 1,000 or so who converted who regretted his decision to leave the Brahminical social order. They were glad to be rid of the abominable caste identity they had carried for so long. They were self-confident and assertive. As a result, no upper caste person dared to disrespect them by calling them derogatory, slanderous names. Their caste identity is a thing of the past.

A similar response was elicited by a good percentage of those who recently embraced Buddhism or Christianity, despite the major stumbling block of the practice of caste within the Christian community (see Chapter Seven). Despite violence, intimidation and a systematic Brahminical conspiracy to remove every personal freedom, the Dalits continue to press for freedom of conscience, the most basic and most valuable of all freedoms given to mankind.

Standing in solidarity with the Dalit movement to embrace other religious ideologies was for India's Christians the essence and a practical demonstration of the Christian view of freedom of conscience. For Christians, freedom of conscience is based on the view of creation, mankind and the free will given to mankind. If Christians really believe in religious liberty and freedom of conscience, then we must give genuine freedom to everyone to choose their own faith or to choose no faith at all. Udit Raj and the Dalit people for the first time asserted their right to choose a faith they believed would deliver them from the clutches of the Hindu caste system. While the apparatus of the State was deployed to prevent these people bonded for 3,000 years to exercise their right of conscience, Christians boldly stood in support of them. We dared to defy the State which infringed upon the personal conscience of the Dalit people.

Our love for the Dalit people is like the love of Christ for them – unconditional. It is not dependent upon them coming to faith in Christ. We love people whether or not they choose to follow Jesus. The Hindutva lie is that Christian love always has an ulterior motive – conversion. We love the Dalit-Bahujan peoples unconditionally. True Christian love is always the agape kind of love – free, unconditional and real. We are able therefore to hold an unwavering faith in the life and teachings of Christ and love all people unconditionally – even our enemies.

Chapter Four
Buddha or Jesus: A Dalit Dilemma

The Dalit exodus toward Islam, Buddhism and Christianity in Haryana where the lynching of the five Dalits took place stunned the nation. It was October 27, 2002, just 12 days after the murder of their fellow Dalits. Udit Raj, the Dalit leader who led the Dalits in embracing Buddhism in 2001, organized a symbolic conversion event for local Dalits who were outraged with the killing of the five young men. On a crowded street corner in the center of town, several hundred Dalit leaders gathered in open revolt. Bollywood film director Mahesh Bhatt (a noted human rights activist), leaders of the Muslim community, and leaders of the All India Christian Council (AICC) were present at this important meeting.

The first Dalit to convert to Islam on that day decided to take "Saddam Hussein" as his new name to demonstrate his rebellion against the caste system. Others became Buddhists as Udit Raj had done earlier.

At the rally, Mr. and Mrs. Chandra Bhan, two bank officers, both Dalits, chose to embrace Christianity. It was their personal choice. They were not forced or coerced into choosing Christ. They were absolutely convinced when they expressed their decision to change their religious identity. There was no ambiguity about what they were doing. They had done their

Dalit families willingly take risks to find freedom

research. Theirs was a carefully considered, final decision. In no uncertain terms they declared they would be following Jesus.

This decision by the Bhan family was not an easy one. They knew there would be consequences. However, they were willing to pay the heavy price for leaving their socio-spiritual system and turning to the Christian faith. They believed that in Christianity they would find dignity and the freedom from caste-based oppression they sought. Though the police continue to harass this couple, they remain steadfast in their decision. In all reality, the wife could lose her job. Their children may lose the affirmative action benefits they now enjoy. Still, this strong-willed family has not wavered in the midst of tremendous pressure and threat.

Dalits like the Bhan family are becoming more willing to endure pressure and threat to find freedom. They take their inspiration from possibly the most highly respected Dalit leader of all time – Dr. B.R. Ambedkar.

In 1956, Ambedkar spearheaded the first major socio-spiritual movement of the Dalit people. He asked them to move away from Hinduism.[18] He was an educated leader who received a doctorate in law in the USA. However, despite his credentials, upon his return to India he found that his social and religious status had not changed in the opinion of caste-minded Hindus. He continued to face caste-based discrimination.

Disgusted by this display of discrimination, Ambedkar led a non-violent revolt against the caste system. He used his influence to ensure that the new Indian Constitution would ban the practice of untouchability. In fact, he tried to banish it completely. Article 17 of the Constitution reads, "Untouchability is abolished and its practice in any form is forbidden. The enforcement of any disability arising out of untouchability shall be an offense punishable in accordance with law." In keeping with this provision, in 1955, the Indian Parliament passed "The Untouchability Offenses Act".

Sadly, though untouchability was banned by the Indian Constitution, the caste system itself was not abolished. The law merely addressed one major symptom of the more serious problem of a caste ideology. Today, the penalties apportioned for caste-based discrimination are enforced rarely because those responsible for enforcing the law are often the upper castes who are themselves biased by caste.

Ambedkar's disillusionment with the inability of the law to deal with the practice of untouchability and its reinforcement of the caste system forced him to look for other religious systems offering the Dalits an escape. At one point he threatened to burn the very Constitution framed under his chairmanship.

His search for another religious way of life began early in his life. He declared that though he was born a Hindu, he would not die a Hindu. His search for an alternative led him to a new version of Buddhism derived from his studies on the birth and growth of Buddhism in India.

During his search, Ambedkar saw clear drawbacks in the Indian Christian Church and in the lives of Christians of his day. Because of this, he considered Christianity not viable for the Dalit people. India was under British rule and the Christianity at that time was closely associated with colonialism.

Ambedkar recognized the fact that Jesus stood out against the caste system. However, he also saw that Indian Christianity had been poisoned by caste-based oppression. He could not accept the fragmented Church which was riddled with its own form of caste-based politics. Ambedkar wanted a religion that would unite his people and bring cohesion to the thousands of sub-castes. He wanted a faith that was willing to work at the

Ambedkar wanted to unite the millions of Dalit people under one religious ideology which gave freedom and dignity

core of society and not at its margins; a faith that was not artificially divided into the "spiritual" and the "non-spiritual". He sought a belief system that affected all areas of Dalit life.

Eventually, Ambedkar chose Buddhism because of its casteless society and unilateral equality. Buddhism as a religion rejected the caste system. Buddha also rejected the Hindu view of three main gods. He rejected idolatry, the idea of reincarnation, and the possibility that he, himself, was an incarnation of God. Buddha gave equality to women.

Despite the success of Ambedkar's embracing Buddhism, the event did not become the greatly anticipated mass exodus out of the Hindu caste system because of the lack of an empowered Dalit leadership during Ambedkar's era. Dalit assertion would take at least another four decades before it would become a major socio-religious force in India. Today, no political party in India can ignore the Dalit movement.

Notes:
18. In 1927, as a protest, Ambedkar burned the law book *Manusmriti* which was against traditional caste restrictions.

Chapter Five
Ambedkar: The Moses of the Dalits

Though Ambedkar's conversion movement did not encompass all Dalits nationwide, the ideology surrounding his Dalit quest for freedom continued to gain strength. Ambedkar's dream for the full freedom of the Dalit people did not happen during his lifetime. However, today, Ambedkar's influence continues to grow in dominance in Indian society. India's current major caste upheaval can be attributed directly to his work and writings. Today's Dalit leadership is strong and motivated to continue Ambedkar's mission.

Udit Raj is one of today's prominent Dalit leaders. He is the Chairman of the All India Confederation of Scheduled Castes/Tribes, an advocacy organization including Government employees, unions and federations. He was born to Dalit parents who were denied a decent life. His given name was Ram Raj. *The Week*, a well-known magazine in India, describes his family conditions best. "Raj hails from a humble family. 'My parents were poor peasants and I had to face tremendous discrimination. We were treated like dirt,' says Raj. Hé adds that he 'always wanted to dedicate his life to the people'."[19] It was this intense desire to help his people that drove Ram Raj to make the most of every opportunity he was given as a young person to improve his life and the life of his family.

As young Ram Raj grew and became educated, he realized the equality that was due to him as a citizen of India. He took advantage of the affirmative action provisions available to him and found a job as an officer in the Indian Revenue Service (IRS), a Government agency.

Ram Raj's passion for his people caused tremendous controversy. However, he knew that he and his compatriots must take a radical stand for their rights as the oppression of the Dalit people continued relentlessly. Casteism locked the Dalits into a life plagued by tyranny of the upper castes.

Through the years, Dalits have been embracing other faiths in various individual states. With a vision to encourage fellow Dalits to leave the caste system, in 2001, Ram Raj and his organization gave a national call to "Quit Hinduism" – an objective they believed would lead Dalits everywhere to find freedom and liberty in other religious systems providing personal dignity and spiritual development. Hinduism could not offer this to the Dalit people.

On November 4, 2001, several thousand Dalits who had arrived the night before, slept in the open air in New Delhi, the capital city of India. They had traveled by bus, by train, and even on foot. Others streamed in throughout the next day from Punjab, Rajasthan, Bihar and Maharashtra. They were making their way to the capital to publicly disown the religion that had for so long rejected them. Most did not know what to expect, but they made the trek anyway, longing for any chance at freedom. They could no longer endure the oppression that had plagued them. They could no longer bear to be the untouchables, unseeables,[20] and unapproachables[21] of Indian society. This day would be their chance to change. This day would be the beginning of social, political and spiritual transformation.

Crowds gathered in Delhi on November 4, 2001, to quit Hinduism

Authorities tried to discourage the Dalit gathering. Approximately 24 hours prior to the event, the police revoked the permission organizers had obtained to conduct the event at the Ram Lila Grounds, a large, popular venue in the heart of New Delhi. Simultaneously, hundreds of thousands of Dalits making their way to the capital were stopped by police and other opponents at state borders. Additionally, some newspapers and posters falsely announced the rally had been cancelled. Threats of violence against Dalits multiplied from extremist Hindu groups.

Initially disheartened, but not deterred, organizers of the event found an alternate location for the event, which ironically also had a sentimental connection. The new location was the Ambedkar Bhavan, a special meeting grounds dedicated to the original savior of the Dalits, Dr. B.R. Ambedkar, who had started the exodus[22] from Hinduism's caste bondage some 50 years earlier.

By mid-morning, the event was underway and tens of thousands of Dalits and interested spectators packed into Ambedkar Bhavan, ready and waiting for the day of transformation to begin. They were seated on the ground, in open windows, on fences and on rooftops. Domestic and international news crews clamored for the best view of this historic ceremony.

"Today this land has taken a bold step! Today we are reborn," declared Raj, who allowed his head to be shaven as part of the "Diksha" (initiation) ceremony. Ram Raj also led the way in changing his first name, "Ram", which was associated with a Hindu god, to "Udit", meaning "arisen". Together with the Buddhist monks who had come to lead these new followers, thousands in the crowd enthusiastically recited the 22 vows of Buddhism. They lifted their hands indicating

Joseph D'souza and Udit Raj in the crowded streets of Delhi on November 4, 2001

their allegiance to their new religion – a religion they were choosing without coercion. It was a religion promising them a sense of personal freedom and equality in return. In addition to the vows they took at the Ambedkar Bhavan, new converts to Buddhism were expected to destroy their idols when they arrived home in their own villages in the days that followed. As one Dalit woman put it, "Millions of gods did not do us any good, so why should we have them at home?" Another repeated Ambedkar's statement: "I was born a Hindu, but I will not die a Hindu."

The Dalits were not alone in their quest for freedom; others actively supported their decision. Representatives of a number of faiths attended the rally in order to express solidarity with the oppressed people's cry for dignity and equality. Three prominent Indian Christian leaders were asked to speak at the rally. One told the crowd of Dalits, "The whole Church of India is with you. We commend you, we are your friends . . . The reason we are here is that Jesus Christ also loves you. He died for you. And we promise that the Church of India will bring you the love of Jesus." This message of the love of God was one the Dalit community had never before heard. Frankly, it was one they had difficulty accepting as true. They had been brainwashed for centuries into thinking that God could not possibly love them. But that day, the Christian leaders assured the Dalit community of the Eternal's unconditional love for them. This perfect love of the Almighty was the thing that could bring perfect freedom. In an interview following the Dalit freedom ceremony, I had the privilege to say to the media, "What happened was incredible: a frontal assault on the caste system and on those who would crush the Dalits' rights. This is a human rights issue. It is our moral duty to stand by the Dalits. If the Church says only one thing, that Jesus Christ loves them, it's the message the Dalit community most needs to hear. They have been told for 3,000 years that God doesn't love them!"

Other non-Christian participants at the rally agreed with the Christian standpoint of solidarity and cooperation with the Dalits. Dr. Kancha Ilaiah of Osmania University, Hyderabad, Andhra Pradesh, stated in support of the Christian standpoint, "Why not? What is wrong if they [Christians] are helping the masses to be spiritually liberated?"

Following Ambedkar's movement into Buddhism in 1956, the Dalit Freedom Ceremony on November 4, 2001, was a second major milestone for the Dalits. This time, however, the Dalits had the support of all sane, secular and non-partisan Indians.

Notes:

19. *The Week*, Nov. 18, 2001, p. 17-18.

20. If unseeables come out during the day, they are said to pollute others just by being visible. Thus, such people are only allowed to come out of their home after sunset and go back home before sunrise.

21. Dalits were expected to maintain a graded distance from the different levels of upper caste people: 33 feet from the lower group; 66 feet from the Brahmins (quoted by Devasahayam 4).

22. In 1956 he led more than three million people out of Hinduism to Buddhism in Maharashtra.

Chapter Six
The Anti-Conversion Conspiracy

Those opposed to Dalit freedom have launched a conspiracy campaign falsely accusing religious leaders of forcibly converting the Dalits. This slanderous accusation is a strategy to put the Christian Church on the defensive for extending a spiritual helping hand to the Dalits and the Other Backward Castes (OBCs). This has resulted in the casteist forces, supported by their militant arms (i.e., Bajrang Dal, Vishwa Hindu Parishad, Hindu Jagran Manch and others), instilling violent fear into the heart and mind of the Church. They want the Church to shut its doors to the oppressed millions who seek holistic liberation and salvation.

This false accusation is primarily intended to demonize the Christian community despite the opponents' failure to produce evidence of cases of forced or fraudulent conversion. The game plan, reminiscent of Nazi propaganda, hinges on repeatedly stating falsehoods until the public believes there must be something suspicious going on about which they do not know.

The media, on the other hand, when they check for illegal conversions, can never find any.

When the brutal attacks against Christians began under the reign of the BJP Government in 1996, the bogey of

69

"conversions" was raised by the leaders of the Hindutva brigade. Christian leaders across the nation were caught unaware both by the viciousness of the attacks by the RSS, the VHP and the Bajrang Dal, and by the tacit political support of these attacks by the ruling BJP Government. After the carnage faced by the churches in the Dangs area of Gujarat in 1998, the BJP Prime Minister called for a national debate on conversions, insinuating that Christian conversions were reason enough for the burning down of churches. The sheer timing of the Prime Minister's utterances again caught the Christians by surprise. Christian leaders argued truthfully that Christian workers were not involved in forced and fraudulent conversions. The civil media picked up the statements of the Christians and some papers castigated the Prime Minister for justifying the violence.

In retrospect, I think we should have challenged the Prime Minister directly, not only for a national debate on conversion, but also in creating a further global debate on Dalit and Backward Caste conversions in India. The Christian Church should have set up the meeting in New Delhi in full view of the national and international media. On one side would be the then Prime Minister and the Sangh Parivar. On the other side would be the followers of Ambedkar, Phule, Periyar and other stalwarts of the Dalit-Bahujan freedom movement. There are enough scholars and spokespersons within the Dalit-Bahujan community to confront the upper caste-led Sangh Parivar. Professor Kancha Ilaiah, Mudra Rakshas, Udit Raj and a host of other leaders could have debated the Parivar and its hate propagandists.

The persecution of Christians has never been about Christians actively engaging in any kind of fraudulent conversions. Modern day Christians oppose such activities because it is opposed to the spirit of Christ. Typically, the persecution of Christians in India has been about the compassionate reception Christians are commanded to give to all those who are oppressed, victimized, violated and dehumanized. The caste system has affected not only the Dalit-Bahujan community in India, but also India's women, irrespective of their caste background. This plight of the Dalits and women across the nation comes from the simple fact that the laws of Manu codified the caste system and made it applicable to everyday life. Christians are persecuted because the Sangh Parivar knows that Christ's message of acceptance, love, affirmation, equality, salvation and transformation is the alternative to the teachings of the caste system.

The Hindutva brigade believes that by using physical force, hate propaganda, institutional harassment, and by passing laws that violate the fundamental rights of human beings, Indian Christians can be intimidated to practice their Christian faith and love only in the confines of their churches.

Leaders from minority groups around India (Dalit, Christian, Buddhist and Muslim) gather to stand against persecution

Instead, exactly the opposite has happened. Christian churches have kept the door wide open to all those who want to enter. Christians continue to live out Jesus' teachings in word and in deed.

Despite their failure to terrorize Indian Christians, the attacks against Christians continue unabated today. The Hindutva forces claim they will not cease until they stop Christian compassionate involvement among the Dalits and oppressed peoples. They say they will fight until Christians quit helping Dalits liberate from an oppressed, untouchable life. The power brokers in Indian society want to maintain the social stagnation in India. The power brokers know that an empowered Dalit-Bahujan population will end the 3,000-year rule of the minority upper caste forces over the majority population.

The upper caste fraternity has no qualms about their children being empowered by Christian education and Christian charity. For instance, they flock to Christian educational institutions in the country. The upper caste leadership in the nation is quick to take advantage of quality, Christian, English-based education, ensuring their future generations will be equipped to be the power brokers in a free India. Those accused of fraudulent conversions must then ask: How many upper caste children have been forcibly converted while studying in Christian schools? The answer? None. Yet, this is the accusation they make when Christians get involved in educating Dalit and OBC children.

As a consequence of the ruling castes' double standard, several new anti-conversion bills were enacted. Of the five anti-conversion bills passed into law, probably the most controversial was passed in the South Indian state of Tamil Nadu where the per capita Christian population is one of the highest

Minority groups across India express solidarity with one another by sharing a common plate

in the nation. Those passing the bill in December 2002 claimed the bill was meant to prevent forced and fraudulent conversions. However, the truth was that the Dalits were willingly and freely embracing other faiths and were facing all the resulting hardships and atrocities.

What the State Government did not anticipate, however, was the response to this unjust law. Everyone quickly realized that the law itself was not against forced or fraudulent conversions. It was a law against Dalits who sought conversion as a way out of the caste maze.

This truth was abundantly demonstrated by the use of the brute force used by the Tamil Nadu State Government to try to stop the December 6, 2002 Dalit protest during which hundreds embraced Christianity and other faiths. The State had not expected the Dalits to stand against the sinister designs of the law. The Dalits knew that this law was meant to forever enslave them in the caste system. They were determined to fight the law and liberate themselves. Despite the law prohibiting them, Dalits in Chennai on that day embraced Christianity and other faiths.

In a shocking turn of events, the reigning State Government in Tamil Nadu lost the 2004 elections. Soon after the election results were announced, the Tamil Nadu anti-conversion law was repealed. The question remains: What happened to the issue of forced and fraudulent conversions? It became immediately obvious to everyone that the Tamil Nadu anti-conversion law had been politically motivated and designed to enslave and intimidate the Dalits who were willingly exiting the caste system into religious faiths offering them freedom and dignity. The repeal of this law was a small, yet significant victory in the battle for Dalit freedom.

The most poignant aspect in the whole debate on conversion across the Indian nation is that there is simply no place in the Christian faith for forced, fraudulent conversions. Jesus never forced anyone to follow Him. God never forces, compels or tricks people into following Him. True discipleship involves a free will decision to follow Jesus and worship Him. Following the example of Jesus, Christians desire to meet the holistic needs of every person around the world so that everyone receives a positive life transformation and an abundance of blessings.

The motive and goal of Indian Christian love is not conversion, but instead to demonstrate the unconditional love of Jesus Christ to the untouchables of India. Christians believe they are commanded to love people and serve them unconditionally whether there is thankfulness or not, whether the recipients follow Christ or not. This is the Christian community's firm stance on the topic of conversion – a stand they intend to maintain until the end.

Chapter Seven
Confronting Caste in the Church

Bangalore, 2001. It was the dawn of the new millennium. Udit Raj's federation and the All India Christian Council (AICC) had organized the gathering and the hall was packed. The traditional oil lamp was lit in front of Dr. B.R. Ambedkar's grand picture, paying homage to a man who is yet to receive the full credit he deserves as one of the towering world socio-spiritual revolutionaries of the twentieth century.

Udit Raj spoke at length against the brutal oppression of the upper castes. He emphasized that without the affirmative action policies enshrined in the Indian Constitution, and without Ambedkar, he would have been sweeping gutters in his home state of Uttar Pradesh, North India. He explained that in the villages and towns of India nothing much had changed even after 50 years of Independence and a Constitution banning untouchability. He lamented that larger society continued its socio-spiritual caste prejudice and discrimination in defiance of the divine law of equality. He said that the way out was to ban the whole caste system and not just deal with its symptoms (i.e., untouchability).

He announced that on November 4, 2001, he would lead hundreds of thousands of people out of Hinduism. "I was born a Hindu, but I will not die a Hindu," he declared, echoing

Ambedkar's statement. A sense of outrage against the caste system filled the hall as he spoke.

I got up to speak. "We are here to express full solidarity with the Dalits and the Backward Castes, and to bear their suffering and pain with them. I believe that now is the hour to draw a firm line against the caste system. We will stand with you and fight with you for your basic rights. Included in this commitment is the desire to empower you in every way we can. We have no ulterior motives. We simply want to demonstrate authentically the love of Christ to your people." I was happy to be able to make such a statement, sure that my colleagues around the nation would stand with me once they understood the full magnitude of the events unfolding before us in a great country like India.

As I finished my statement and sat down, I noticed that Mr. V.T. Rajshekar, a fierce spokesperson of the Dalit cause, got up. He came to the stage. He wanted to respond to my statement. My heart sank as I knew what was to come.

Unflinchingly, he attacked the caste system within the Church in India and asked if there was any initiative to do anything about it. He wondered why it had taken the Indian Christian community so long to take a public stand of solidarity with the Dalits and Backward Castes. He wondered whether the persecution by the Hindutva forces had anything to do with our seemingly fresh posture. He questioned the depth of our commitment to the Dalit-Bahujan people.

After his backlash, however, he welcomed our support. The global community must join the battle to deal with the evils perpetuated by the caste system. The Christian community should mobilize global opinion against caste discrimination. He expressed his concern that the upwardly mobile English-educated elite of the upper castes trotting around the globe working in the world of information technology and business was ill-suited to speak out on the injustices within Indian society. Who had the courage to speak against the full-blown slavery of the caste system in India?

Sitting on my chair on the stage, I realized there was no point in defending the sin the Indian Christian Church had been committing for centuries. One thing was crystal clear: Caste discrimination within the Church was a shame and stigma to the life and message of Jesus. It was a betrayal of Jesus' mission itself.

I admitted that the Church in India was in the wrong and needed to repent. I admitted that the caste system was antithetic to Jesus' teachings about the Kingdom of God. I admitted that we had nothing to say in our defense and that we

The Christian Church pledges full solidarity with the Dalits and desires to eradicate caste from the Church

as the body of Indian believers should ask for the forgiveness of the Dalit-Bahujan people. I promised to wait for every opportunity to demonstrate in a tangible way that we love the Dalit-Bahujan people and want to care for them. I explained that all human beings are made equal in the image of God. There is no such thing as the superior Brahmin and the inferior Dalit. I stressed the fact that Indian Christians must agree with Ambedkar's thesis in his "Annihilation of Caste" (see Appendix Seven).

I am ashamed that the caste system has penetrated the Church in India. The caste system surpasses white racial apartheid in its sheer evil against humanity. There is no real escape from the caste system. There is no upward mobility. Financial prosperity, though welcome, does not remove the stigma of caste. For caste-minded Hindus, Dalits do not deserve to prosper. Their lack of dignity is innate in their very existence. It is therefore the right of the upper caste to oppress the lower castes and Dalits. I have stated previously that the caste system and its attitudes make the Dalits the supreme victims of human civilization.

The fact that the caste system still survives on the globe and oppresses people is a dark blot against human civilization. Women, the Sudras (lowest caste), and the Dalits – the vast majority of people in India – are confined socially and theologically to the status of lesser human beings by virtue of birth. God is said to have created them unequal. Every sub-caste (over 6,000 of them) is placed in a divine hierarchy through birth. This caste system, codified by Manu over 3,000 years ago, surely surpasses everything else in the history of man's cruelty and oppression against fellow human beings.

At the human level, the roots of the caste system lie in the dark side of mankind which is utterly selfish, evil and without remorse. The dark side of man is capable of constructing and ordering religion and God in such a way that it justifies man's violence against his fellow man. It is capable of creating the collective conscience that legitimizes evil and blatant injustice. Man's unwillingness to accept his true position in relation to his fellow man is the driving passion behind this and every other social evil. Social evil only portrays evil against the Divine. In this context, the pretext of religious traditions and practices is meaningless. Any saintliness, divine "enlightenment", or God-experience devoid of concurrent social justice and righteousness in all spheres of human life denies the essence of true religion. Sin against man is a sin against the Divine. By subscribing to the evils of caste, the Church in India is sinning against God.

Having learned and experienced the love of God, the Indian Church should know that the fundamental equality of all human beings is a self-evident truth. Equality is intrinsic to the makeup of mankind, however downtrodden and oppressed. Modern genetic science has underscored the fact that we are children of the same stock and that underneath, the color of all our skin is identical – and ultimately it is discolored by sin. Tragically, the Indian Church has not yet learned this full lesson. More than 50 years ago, the Christian Church failed Ambedkar and his people. We should have shown solidarity with that movement because those were very difficult times. Today, unless there is tremendous reformation, the Church will again betray the Dalit-Bahujan peoples.

If the Indian Church engages in this huge socio-spiritual reformation happening within Indian society, its impact will be felt not only in India, but also around the world. This dynamic movement will compel Christians everywhere to respond authentically to a world filled with pain, injustice and moral degradation. The Church must therefore respond in earnest to a world looking for authentic spirituality.

It is time for the Indian Church to act. It will not have another chance to redeem itself.

Chapter Eight
Agenda for Dalit Spiritual Emancipation

The Dalits are looking for socio-spiritual freedom, equality and dignity. They are determined to find a way of escape. The idea of Dalit freedom has come and is here to stay. What should we do?

1. The first item on the Dalit Freedom agenda must be dialogue with the Dalit leadership. Since the landmark meeting with the Dalit leadership in 2001, the Christian community in India has expressed its genuine desire to stand alongside the Dalit people as they work their agenda for emancipation. It is because of this consistent interaction with the Dalit community, that Dalits have extended an invitation to the Christians to assist them in their quest. Many hundreds of meetings have taken place between Christians and Dalit-Bahujan leaders. It has been my privilege to speak out against Dalit atrocities, to march with Dalit-Bahujan leaders as they protested against discrimination and atrocities, and to speak to tens of thousands of them all over the nation and overseas.

All the strategic programs in place today exist as a result of direct interactions, suggestions and requests from the Dalit leadership. We do not initiate the programs. The Dalit-Bahujan community does.

2. The Dalit leaders want to see their children get a quality, English-based (plus mother-tongue) education with an alternate worldview teaching them they are made in the image of God. God loves every Dalit. He does not want to punish them for being born into a particular caste. Every individual can have full spiritual freedom and can experience the blessings and forgiveness of God. They, too, have the right to become priests. They can achieve their full potential in this life, and birth does not determine their future status.

According to many Dalit leaders, offering a world class English education with an alternate worldview will change the Dalit situation permanently. Udit Raj says, "Caste inferiority must be taken out of the minds of our children and our people. That is where the main work must be done."

*Dalits want to leave behind traditional work and
join in the global marketplace*

Education is one of the keys to Dalit freedom

Dalit leaders want education that will bring their children to the academic level of others in the top schools across the nation to compete with their upper caste peers. They need teachers who care for each child's emotional and academic needs. They need an English-based education so they can compete in a global economy. They must have the opportunity to earn a globally recognized education, and therefore have the chance to participate in the new globalized marketplace.

Participation in the global economy is a serious issue for India's Dalits. In the new Indian economy, globalization and information technology have not yet reached the Dalits. Companies do not currently have English-language training programs for uneducated Dalits. Potential workers must speak English and have minimum computer skills. Without these things, Dalits may never be hired.

Education and employment being correlated, we find that the majority of privatized public sector companies today are owned and operated by the elitist upper castes. Where is the Dalit entrepreneur who owns a public sector company that has gone private in the process of liberalization? Unfortunately they do not exist.

In the era of privatization, liberalization and globalization, once again it is the upper caste minority that has the largest portion of the cake. The rest who are outside of the economic system are left to live on the crumbs. The poor have become poorer. Absolute poverty has increased due to the operation of unequal forces in the global market. Democracy means a level playing field for all. Democracy means a Dalit could genuinely aspire to become the Prime Minister of India because it is in the realm of reality and not "maya" or illusion.

Tragically, India is the land where only the powerful minority participates in the economic power game. They have a monopoly and reap the benefits. The majority who are poor and the outcastes of society are spectators watching the good life from a distance. Television screens flicker images of a lifestyle beyond the imagination of many lower caste people. Farmers commit suicide in many parts of India. A nation that boasts millions of tons of surplus grain has severe starvation problems in Orissa, Gujarat and Rajasthan. While the upper castes "shine", the Dalits are left to their centuries-old fate. The upper castes in the cities of India enjoy the fruits of the expanding global economy. The Dalits, however, are completely excluded. Dalits simply do not qualify to enter the global market.

Dalit betterment comes from education. It is knowledge that creates all other avenues for freedom. Education is one of the keys to any advancement the Dalits hope to have in this world. The Christian community in India, therefore, has accepted the Dalit invitation to provide education. They want education for Dalit children, literacy for adults, vocational training for both men and women, and micro-enterprise for those who already have marketable skills. It is education and training that will make a lasting impact. For Dalits, education is the way forward.

Since 2001, this education comes in the form of Dalit Education Centers. Hundreds of these Centers are running across the nation. These are schools created for the basic purpose of bringing freedom and betterment to the Dalit people. The teachers in each of these schools have a personal vision for empowering the Dalits. After the primary education is completed, every effort is made to move each Dalit child into higher-level English medium schools in the vicinity of their village

Dalit Education Centers give Dalit children an English education

or community. Some of them will graduate from these schools in 2009. Amazingly, this is just five years away. In five years, there will be Dalit children qualified to get entry-level jobs with a global language at their command. They could also go for university-level studies. A small section of Dalit youth will, outside the affirmative action system, have the opportunity to break free from the caste barriers that have handicapped them for thousands of years.

　　3. The Dalit Freedom agenda also includes working with the Dalit/OBC leaders to find an alternate spiritual ideology that counters the system of oppression. I am deeply aware of the complexity of caste tensions and strife and how politicians have manipulated these differences.

　　As a Christian, I believe Jesus' life and message is the perfect fit for the Dalit-Bahujan quest for socio-spiritual freedom. Jesus is the Peacemaker between communities. He is also the Peacemaker between God and man. He is the One who gives full equality, dignity, freedom and spiritual rights to all. The Dalit-Bahujan peoples have the right to know these things. They need to know what options they have in choosing an alternate socio-spiritual ideology.

　　Thus, I also believe that the Dalit-Bahujan peoples should be completely free to make their own individual choices. I do not want to impinge on their freedom of conscience. Why should anyone have objection to this? Does not God love people unconditionally? Does not Jesus love the Dalit-Bahujan peoples?

　　This alternate spiritual ideology is truly a key issue in the Dalit Freedom agenda. The Dalit/OBC leaders insist that an alternate spiritual ideology must challenge the spiritual ideology on which caste is based – Brahminism. The alternate ideology must offer them the full spiritual rights denied to them thus far. Christian and non-Christian thinkers in India have argued that the key to achieving full Dalit-Bahujan freedom and transformation is embracing an alternate spiritual ideology.

Dr. Kancha Ilaiah is a Bahujan (member of the low, backward castes). He is a highly respected teacher within intellectual circles in India and in the ecumenical religious community. His opinions and writings about the atrocities faced by the low castes, backward castes and Dalits have become popular and also controversial on the Indian national scene because they clearly lay blame on the Brahmin-based socio-spiritual society which creates the conditions of caste oppression. He calls the Hindu caste system and its political results a form of spiritual fascism – totalitarianism – a one-party government, run by the minority Brahmins, requiring complete subservience under the reigning powers. It is this spiritual fascism that has controlled political power and shaped India down through the centuries, according to Ilaiah. It is this ideology that must be replaced by an alternate ideology giving dignity and equality to all (see Appendix Two).

For Ilaiah, this alternate ideology must begin through education and through access to the priesthood. He claims that one of the main reasons for Dalit oppression is the upper castes' religious and educational domination through the requirement of Sanskrit in religious activities. In the modern period, they exercise power through their monopoly of English-based schools, and by prohibiting Dalit-Bahujans from becoming Hindu priests. By maintaining control in these areas, the Dalits are left with no option but to be confined to their untouchability and backwardness. Ilaiah says, "They [the Scheduled Castes] must be given a ceremonial apology in all temples of India for being kept untouchable. If the priestly class does not do that, it has no right to tell the people not to embrace Christianity or any other religion that wants to give them the right to priesthood and the power to control religious institutions."[23]

Further, if Dalits are given full social, political and spiritual rights within the Hindu caste system, Ilaiah opines, "One family will operate as a unit of multi-cultural and economic skills. The productivity, creativity and spirituality operate in a language of communicability in the family, community (not caste) and also the village. If an untouchable becomes a priest who can command respect in every home, he should not recreate the culture of the priest. He/she should be a democratic representative of the spiritual agency who talks your language, who drinks your water and who eats your cooked food."[24]

Despite Ilaiah's ideological suggestions, the fact remains that the ideology of the Hindu caste system will not change in such an optimistic manner. The Brahmins will not easily relinquish power. The worldview of the Hindu caste system will not change in such a way that it releases millions of people from its clutches. The ties to the very personhood of the caste Hindu are simply too deep. According to Mudra Rakshas' latest book on interpreting the Hindu Scriptures, the socio-spiritual liberation of the Dalit-Bahujans simply cannot take place within the Hindu caste system. Leaders like Mahatma Phule, Dr. Ambedkar and Periyar Ramasamy insisted that the upper caste hierarchy stands to lose a lot if the caste structure is dismantled. However, India as a nation stands to gain an immense amount if its people are fully and finally freed from the evils of caste. India will occupy its rightful place in the world once the fsDalit-Bahujan peoples are completely free, live in full personal dignity, and have dignity in labor.

The genetic ability of Indians is first-class as displayed by the millions of Indians who live outside India. Indians have talent, they work hard, and they can compete with the world's

Dalits are ready and waiting to be trained to work in the fields of technology, medicine, engineering and law

best if they have equal opportunity and human dignity. But Indian society (as opposed to the Constitution) is not a place of equal opportunity and dignity even today. Let us not be fooled by the "India Shining" slogan of the Indian cities. The cities do not represent India. True India lives in the inlands of our great nation. The villages, small towns and rural areas are what represent the heart and soul of India. These places are where the majority low castes and Dalits live.

This is where a Dalit who aspires to cross the labor boundaries as defined by caste loses his life. A Dalit Christian lady doctor in Lakhimpur Kheri, Uttar Pradesh, is forced to sweep the floors and clean the toilets of her hospital by upper caste hoodlums who challenge her audacity to choose a career in medicine. This profession is meant only for the upper castes, they assert.

If Ambedkar had not fought for reservations and reserved constituencies (affirmative action) for the Dalits, we would not today have any Dalits in the higher levels of government. We would not have about five million Dalits working in the government. All jobs, except those that come under the occupation of the untouchables, would have been taken by the elitist castes.

The great tragedy of India is that Brahmins did not take up a nationwide battle against the caste system. Mahatma Phule mourned this fact and pointed out to the nation the example of America where white Americans led the fight against racism.

Ambedkar argued that the Brahmins would never battle with the caste system as it would threaten their very existence and political power base. Instead, in the political realm, Dalits have been co-opted into upper caste political parties. Dalit Members of Parliament (barring some exceptions) serve as mere tokens of political involvement without actual power. The major political parties are often bastions of upper caste power and Dalit tokenism.

Having said these things, today there are plenty of progressive Brahmins and upper caste people who detest the caste system and want to eradicate caste disease. Many Brahmin women support the liberation movement of the downtrodden castes. Why? It is because they have also suffered under the laws of Manu.

A frontal combined challenge to the caste system is waiting to happen. The power brokers in society will stop at nothing to maintain the present structure. Those battling the caste system know that the power brokers will use violence to stop the Dalit quest for freedom.

Mahatma Gandhi struggled nobly to remove the evil symptoms of caste discrimination. He tried to be an example himself. His mistake, however, was believing that the inhuman discrimination of the caste system would be eliminated if untouchability were banned by the Constitution.

But fifty years later, untouchability and caste discrimination have not vanished. Yes, some would argue that there are some changes. But the deep-rooted problem has not yet been solved. In fact, atrocities against Dalits increase by the day.

How would Gandhi feel today if he knew that the very word "Harijan" he created to give dignity to the untouchables has become a derogatory word Dalits abhor? The very forces that killed him are today in full bloom. The casteist Hindutva regime destroys the very notion of the pan-Indian consciousness which Gandhi tried to leave as his legacy to the nation. Did Gandhi ever envision the forces of the Sangh Parivar demolishing the concept of Indian-ness for which he gave his life? What is the new Hindu nationalism except the emergence of caste-based Hinduism that relegates the Dalits, the minorities, the Backward Castes and the tribal people to their ordained positions as second or third class citizens in India? Why did no one in the power structure of the Sangh Parivar challenge the Vice President of the VHP and his completely insane comments about Dalits after the lynching? (See page 29.)

Some politicians state that religion will not effectively remove the caste system. These politicians need to once again read Ambedkar and Mahatma Phule. This viewpoint also reveals the moral bankruptcy of these politicians. It does not matter to which religion they belong. As a class, these politicians have failed miserably the Dalit-Bahujan peoples.

4. Next on the Dalit-Bahujan agenda is to tackle the constant violation of the human rights of Dalit men, women and children. Those who are concerned about the illegal trafficking of women must realize that in India the majority of them come from the Dalits and lower castes. Those who are concerned about bonded child labor must understand that the majority of the bonded child laborers in India are from the Dalit and Backward Castes. Words cannot adequately express the atrocities carried out against Dalit women. Dalits say they are untouchable except when it comes to their girls and women who are frequently raped, abused and killed. Nothing less than a global movement is going to end this state of affairs. The local upper caste power brokers will not yield or change unless there is a non-violent but sacrificial and peaceful revolt against the system.

Dalit leaders have pointed out that when the Brahminical forces attacked Indian Christians there was protest and action in India and all over the world. Yet when Dalits are attacked and forced to face worse atrocities almost daily, no one notices or protests.

The Dalit leaders are absolutely correct. The time has come to protest, write, campaign, and notify the nation and world when Dalits are attacked, abused, raped and victimized. There must be a unified national and global campaign against the victimization of the Dalits.

5. **We also must affirm and redeem all aspects of Dalit-Bahujan culture.** In addition to 1) dialogue, 2) education, 3) an alternate spiritual ideology, and 4) Dalit human rights, the preservation of genuine Dalit-Bahujan culture will bring signficant change. When Brahminical interpreters of Indian society talk about Indian culture, they refer to the culture of Brahminism. This is not the same as Dalit-Bahujan culture as ideologues are noting. The Dalit Freedom agenda aims to preserve and affirm all aspects of Dalit culture beginning with the dignity of labor, their music, their history, their art, their indigenous science, and even their food. We want to see Dalit communities allowed to reach their full potential.

Dalit-Bahujan culture must be preserved and affirmed

I like the term that is used by Dalit-Bahujan leaders: "The Dalitization of Indian society". There are so many precious cultural, social and spiritual aspirations in the Dalit-Bahujan societies that we must capture, affirm and redeem.

If we work for the abolition of the caste system, then we are true followers of the Phule/Ambedkar heritage. Anything less will not do. Both Indian society and the world community must learn and understand the gravity of the Dalit condition. Discrimination based on descent qualifies as religiously-sanctioned racism and should therefore be included as an issue of global concern. The treatment of the Dalits violates every code of human rights known to human history. The international voice can make a difference. A strong national and international movement can help eradicate this sub-human system.

6. *Finally, we want to work toward affirmative action for the Dalits in the global economy.* For at least the next 25 years, Dalits must be given equal opportunities through affirmative action in the global marketplace. The response of the Indian industry barons to the present Prime Minister's call for affirmative action for the Dalits is extremely disappointing and depressing. We urge multinational companies who have their investments and presence in India, especially those from the USA, to take stock of this issue and initiate appropriate and relevant policies. We ask them to engage in English-medium education for the Dalits at all levels. The mental ability of the Dalits is first class. Let us open up the global market for the Dalit-Bahujan peoples.

Notes:
23. Kancha Ilaiah, *Spiritual Fascism and Civil Society*, p. 18.
24. Ibid.

Chapter Nine
Jesus and Brahminism

Mahatma Phule pointed out 150 years ago that British Christianity in India was not living up to the teachings of Christ even as it allowed the Brahminical forces to interpret both India and caste-based Hinduism. In his book *Slavery*, he attacked the British powers for withdrawing the teachings of the Bible from the Indian schools. This curriculum had become a source of teaching on human equality and spiritual democracy. It was destined to make a positive difference in Indian society. However, the British rulers could not withstand the pressure of the Brahminical forces in Maharashtra, and withdrew the teachings of the Bible from the classrooms.

Mahatma Phule correctly stated that the teachings of Jesus would unleash powerful forces of socio-spiritual liberation movements within the Dalit-Bahujan communities in India. Caste-based discrimination, oppression and victimization cannot derive any support from what Jesus taught and from what He did on the Cross.

On the Cross, Jesus became the ultimate victim of injustice, facing the abuse of both religious and State power. Those who victimized Him could not tolerate Jesus' idea that all human beings are equal before God, that God created no difference between the races, and that He allowed all people to

95

have equal liberation, salvation, opportunities and blessings from Him. He smashed the notion of human mediators between God and mankind. He spoke against the monopoly of the priestly class in religious matters. In short, Jesus' message and life were a complete antithesis to Brahminism.

At the Cross, spiritual fascism was dealt a death blow as spiritual rights were extended to all people freely and equally – namely, the right of access to God in this life through forgiveness of sins, the right of free access to places of worship, and the right of access to the priesthood for all. Jesus demolished once for all the social and racial boundaries that divided people. He inaugurated a new humanity, a new community on earth. The Cross condemns and rejects discrimination based on race, descent or religion.

At the Cross, Jesus ensured the full and final victory of all victims. His death signaled victory over oppressive forces of victimization, both spiritual and physical. Simply put, at the Cross, Jesus "the crucified, innocent victim" was declared Lord of all. God gave all power to the Ultimate Victim. Ever since Jesus' crucifixion, the voice of this Victim refuses to be silenced in world history. He became Savior and Lord of the human race by dying — not by killing.

The Cross was to have tremendous impact on the course of history as victims of all oppression have found impetus and inspiration from the Cross to carry on their struggle for freedom and justice through non-violent means. Death itself was no more an object of fear in order to achieve spiritual freedom, liberation and justice. Jesus generated courage and confidence in death and in suffering.

The Cross of Christ is the place of forgiveness, shelter, liberation, acceptance and hope for the Dalits and all the oppressed. The Cross of Christ is also the place where

Brahminism meets its judgment and condemnation.

Who would have thought that Jesus' struggle with the religious leaders of his day – the Pharisees and the Sadducees – would parallel so closely the struggle against Brahminism? The Pharisees as a religious class exhibited most of the features of the Brahminism of India. These are the same characteristics against which Ambedkar and others so fiercely fought. Consider the following points of similarity.

First, Jesus refused to ban anyone from access to God and the temple. When the Samaritan woman met Jesus she was astonished that Jesus would actually talk to her. She was an untouchable of her day. She could not go to the temple where she thought she could meet and worship God. She was considered a polluted sinner. Yet Jesus reached out to her. He

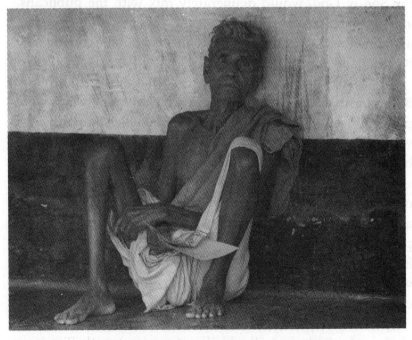

In Jesus, Dalits are no longer victimized

accepted her and let her know that God would forgive all her sins and completely embrace her. Her background (i.e., her caste) was not a barrier since she was a child of God like everyone else. This personal interaction with Jesus completely changed the Samaritan woman's life.

Brahminism continues to insist on the notion that only the priestly caste has access to the main temples and to God, and that Brahmins are the highest form of human life innate with inborn purity. The Dalits and the Backward Castes do not have this status and thus are destined to a life with no real access to God.

Second, Jesus mingled with the dregs of society, the poor, the sinners and those who were considered polluted. The Pharisees simply could not digest that Jesus, who claimed to be the Son of God, would deliberately mix with the publicans, sinners, outcasts and rejects of society. He met with them, ate and dined with them, and talked to them about the coming new Kingdom of God.

The Pharisees and Sadducees, like those who follow Brahminism, had a clear idea about which human beings were pure, righteous and acceptable to God, and which human beings were not. The Pharisees dared not mix with polluted people or be seen in their company.

Jesus fiercely challenged this attitude with His new vision of the Kingdom where all people are made in the image of God and where the God of love reaches out to the oppressed, the poor, the sinners and the downtrodden. This concept of the Kingdom of God is directly opposed to the tenets of Brahminism which preordains people based on sins committed in a past life, condemning them to a caste prison forever.

Third, Jesus introduced and emphasized the concept of God as the Father of all. In direct contrast with Pharisaic teaching and Brahminism, Jesus taught that God was actually the Father of all human beings. This means we all come from one Father God. None of us come from His feet and none of us are the unborn or the untouchable. There is no such thing as a preordained hierarchy of human beings.

The Pharisees and Sadducees, like the Brahminical teachers, found this doctrine tormenting. Suddenly, in the new Kingdom of God, Jesus pronounced there was equality for all of us in relation to God. Jesus stated that every human being was an equal child of God and could authentically call God His Father. Father God loves all of us equally. When the Pharisees saw that Jesus was eating with the outcasts and tax collectors, they asked His disciples, "Why does He eat with such people?" Jesus heard them and answered, "*People who are well do not need a doctor, but only those who are sick. I have not come to respectable people, but outcasts*" (Mark 2:17).

Fourth, Jesus rejected the notion that some people face today's oppression because of sins committed in a past life. At one time Jesus' disciples asked Him about a man who was handicapped. They wondered whether it was because the man was more sinful than others. Jesus rejected this concept because Jesus knew that in God's eyes we are all equally sinners who need His love, grace and forgiveness. God knows no man is perfect. He knows that no Brahmin or Pharisee is less of a sinner than any other person in the human race.

Jesus clearly taught that God was completely impartial and did not have favorites. If He did have favorites, then they were the oppressed, the poor, the needy, and the sinful who look to Him for grace, help and forgiveness.

Jesus completely rejected the notion that our fate in this

life is determined by sins in a past life. He rejected the idea of a past life altogether. He clearly emphasized that all we have is the present life and the life to come in the Kingdom of God. Jesus knew that the notions of evils done in a past life could be used to oppress and burden the poor, the needy and the guilty.

Fifth, Jesus refused the notion that man needs a human mediator to connect with God, Through their teaching and resulting lifestyle, the Pharisees and Sadducees earned money and power by becoming mediators between God and man. Brahminism also has thrived on this teaching. Thus, India has a temple economy and a politicized religion.

Jesus told the Samaritan woman and others that through Jesus, God is available to every human being in his own heart. Mankind does not need a human mediator. Jesus, through His

In Jesus, Dalits do not need a mediator between God and mankind.

death on the Cross, shattered the need for a human mediator. Once for all through achieving the acceptance of God and the forgiveness of sins, man can approach God directly in his heart. There is no need for temple sacrifice. No need to bribe God.

By teaching this ideology and then insisting on its application, Jesus shook the very foundation of the Pharisaic religious system. The Pharisees knew that this teaching was revolutionary and their days of power over people were numbered. The same teaching is a direct challenge to Brahminism. We do not need a priestly class to mediate between mankind and God. We can all have direct access to God. We can all become priests. In fact, we can all become the temple of God.

Sixth, Jesus taught that we should be loyal citizens, as well as loyal worshipers of God. The Pharisees and Sadducees, like Brahminism today, tried to confuse the lines between the worship of God and the duties of the citizen to the State. One day they tried to trap Jesus by asking him whether it was right for people to pay taxes to the Government. Jesus' classic answer was that we should give to Caesar what is Caesar's and to God what is God's. No one should confuse the two. As citizens of any country, we should give to the nation all that the nation rightly requires of us. We should be patriotic. We should be nation builders. We should work for development, peace and communal harmony. We should work for justice and righteousness.

At the same time, we should give to God what is God's. Only God deserves to be worshiped by human beings. Only God has the power to destroy or preserve our soul. Jesus saw no contradiction between the two realms.

But Pharisaical teaching and Brahminism both attempt to create this tension between faith and the State. The

*True religion takes care of those in need
and gives dignity to all forms of labor*

Brahminical Hindutva project is designed to force us to agree with Brahminism. They say those who do not agree are not true Indians. This is insidious teaching and propaganda.

Finally, Jesus' definition of true religion was different from the Brahminical idea of religion. Jesus challenged the Pharisees and Sadducees on the nature of true religion. According to the Pharisees, it was all about wearing certain clothes, doing certain rituals, and following innumerable rules on purity and sacrifice. Further, religion was about words, more words, and religious festivals and events. Conversely, Jesus said true religion exists in the practice of faith. He said that faith without works of righteousness, justice and compassion was dead.

True religion is about taking care of those who are robbed and left on the road. True religion is about giving water to those who are thirsty. It is about providing food for the hungry, sight for the blind, care for the sick, and encouragement for the dying and bereaved. It is about cleaning the body of the leper, living with the untouchables of society, and bringing communities together. True religion is about being peacemakers rather than violence creators, standing up for the powerless in society, protecting the rights of women and children, and joining hands with all those who are doing good and standing in solidarity with the oppressed, the victimized and the forsaken. True religion in India is embracing the Dalits who have remained untouchable for centuries.

As we consider the above, we can see clearly why the perpetrators of Brahminism have counted Jesus as their supreme enemy in India's current turmoil. Jesus was not bothered about the Pharisees and the Sadducees. He knew they would kill Him because of this. He was prepared to die. He knew this teaching was costly and would involve suffering. Just, righteous and non-violent revolutions are costly. Similarly, Jesus would not have bothered about the Brahminical and Hindutva forces. He is on a path to embrace all Dalits of India. He is on a course to sit with them and eat whatever is available in their huts.

As Jesus demonstrated with the Pharisees and Sadducees, Brahminism must be countered by all Indians on an ideological basis. Like Jesus, who challenged Pharisaic religion, we should not be afraid to speak out on behalf of justice and truth. The main weapon we have is the truth and its power to dismantle all falsehood.

If the upper caste leadership and even sections in the Church are irritated by our stand, so be it. We need to show great fortitude and courage. Like Jesus, we should intentionally mix with the Dalit-Bahujan community in our social and economic interaction. Inter-caste marriages must be supported. Our practice in daily life should challenge the inequities in our society.

Like Jesus, we should also be non-violent in our challenge of Brahminism. We cannot counter hate with hate or violence with violence. The oppressor is often the one who is in the most needy state because he can evolve into a human monster.

Brahminism and extremist Hindutva forces killed the Father of the Nation, Mahatma Gandhi. Gandhi's life was impacted enormously by Jesus' Sermon on the Mount. He tried his best to reform the system and build a genuine sense of pan-Indian nationhood. The same Hindutva forces burned Graham Staines and his sons. The same forces engaged in genocide in Gujarat a couple of years ago.

Like Jesus, Gladys Staines, the widow of the martyred Graham who worked among the untouchables, openly forgave her husband's killers. Stephen, the first martyr of the Church, publicly forgave the Pharisees and other religious leaders of his day as they were killing him. Jesus stated on the cross, "Father, forgive them for they know not what they do."

Therefore, like Jesus, we must use the power of truth and justice on the one hand, and combine it with the power of love on the other side. Nothing can withstand this divine combination of forces.

Jesus knew, of course, that death was not going to be the end. He knew it was in His death and resurrection that He would carry His vision of the Kingdom of God into true and lasting fulfillment. In His resurrection, the Dalits of India will also resurrect. India as a nation is in the process of its ultimate rebirth.

Chapter Ten
A True Story of Dalit Freedom

Decades ago, in a small village in rural Gujarat, a young boy named Mojis sat at his mother's feet, listening to her narrate the story of a man who had become Mojis' hero: his grandfather. Mojis' grandfather, who also lived in rural Gujarat, was a Dalit. The man and his family knew generations of oppression, generations of atrocity. However, throughout the years, the family had embraced the teachings of Jesus Christ and found freedom and comfort in His teachings and lifestyle.

One unexpected evening, however, hoodlums broke into the family's humble home and began attacking them. The attackers opposed the Christianity Mojis' grandfather's family had embraced. They opposed the freedom these Dalit people had found outside the caste system. In the midst of the attack, the family – eight in all – fled. They ran away, losing track of each other, never to have contact again.

Mojis' grandfather fled to a medium-sized town, hoping to find refuge in the larger population. He married, but then died within just a few years. He never had the chance to pass his Christian faith on to his family, but the values of human worth and dignity that Christianity promotes formed his young family's ethos.

Devastated by her husband's death, Mojis' grandmother was forced to go to work. She found work in a cotton mill. As a Dalit, this backbreaking manual labor was her only option. She worked hard and was barely able to earn enough money to provide food, clothing and shelter for her children. Education, however, was not possible. Thus, their desperate plight drew the sympathy of local residents who helped the children in her family get an English-based education. The widow's son (who would one day grow up to be Mojis' father) was the first Dalit in the local area to complete a high school education. The family was thrilled at the opportunity for transformation this accomplishment represented.

Soon after his graduation, his widowed mother arranged a marriage for her son to a young Dalit woman who had also been fortunate enough to be educated through Grade Seven and then trained as a nurse. The two married and began providing free medical help to local Dalit people. They became respected in their town for their acts of selfless kindness. However, they never lost their identity as Dalits.

This status as the untouchables of society followed them wherever they went. Even in the homes of their upper caste "friends", they were served disposable clay cups for drinking water or tea. The man and his wife had children, one of whom was Mojis, and these children were not allowed by society to invite upper caste children into their home to play, or even to share a drink of water on the hottest of summer days. Mojis grew up being teased and tormented because of his Dalit identity. He was bullied at school and on the playground. He was mocked and demeaned. Even today as a grown man, when Mojis returns to his village, he is offered a drink only in a clay cup.

Often, Mojis would arrive home after an incident with the upper caste children with tears streaming down his face.

Like other Dalits, Mojis was forced to drink in disposable cups

He would run to his mother for comfort and assurance. It was during those precious times that Mojis' mother would pull him onto her lap, cradle him in her arms and remind him of his Creator. Over the years, Mojis' mother and father had embraced Christianity, as Mojis' grandfather had done a generation before. Mojis' mother found her identity in the values of Christ and she wanted to pass that identity to her own children. She encouraged Mojis in these times of heartbreak by telling him that God loved him and had created him for a unique purpose. She prayed that God would comfort Mojis and help him to feel the dignity innate in his very existence. She even opened the Bible and turned to the pages where Mojis' name (English translation: Moses) appeared. "Look!" she exclaimed. "God thinks you are so important that He even put your name in His book!"

It was this love and assurance of both his mother and the living God that helped form Mojis' worldview. Even though the caste-based society in which he lived confined him to a life of ridicule and oppression, damaging his self-worth, his positive Christian upbringing convinced him there was something greater planned for him. He knew there was a God who valued him, who loved him, and who had an exciting plan for his days ahead.

Mojis was born a Dalit and suffered oppression at the hands of high caste villagers as a child. Today, however, Mojis is one of the senior leaders in a widely-known, indigenous, non-profit organization. Because of his childhood experiences, Mojis greatly sympathizes with the plight of the Dalits and works on their behalf across the nation. He and his staff work to empower the oppressed and bring full-life transformation.

On a recent overseas trip to England for a leadership conference, Mojis sat before a computer terminal taking a personality inventory that would determine his leadership style. After answering more than 200 in-depth questions about his upbringing and worldview, the inventory returned a surprising result. The inventory indicated that Mojis must have been born into a privileged family with a positive, empowered upbringing producing a psychologically sound and progressive lifestyle today. There was no evidence of the oppression he faced as a child. Caste inferiority in his mind and lifestyle had been fully conquered. Mojis had truly experienced a full-life transformation in one generation.

Dalit Freedom is possible – Now and Forever.

Appendix One
Why Conversion?
by Dr. B.R. Ambedkar
Used with Permission

Class Struggle

There are two aspects of conversion; social as well as religious; material as well as spiritual. Whatever may be the aspect or line of thinking, it is necessary to understand the beginning, the nature of untouchability and how it is practiced. Without this understanding, you will not be able to realize the real meaning underlying my declaration of conversion. In order to have a clear understanding of untouchability and its practice in real life, I want you to recall the stories of the atrocities perpetrated against you. But very few of you might have realized as to why all this happens! What is at the root cause of their tyranny? To me it is very necessary that we understand it.

This is not a feud between rival men. The problem of untouchability is a matter of class struggle. It is the struggle between caste Hindus and the Untouchables. This is not a matter of doing injustice against one man. This is a matter of injustice being done by one class against another. This "class struggle" has a relation with the social status. This struggle indicates how one class should keep its relation with another class. This struggle starts as soon as you start claiming equal treatment with others.

Conversion not for Slaves

The reason for their anger is very simple. Your behaving on par with them insults them. Untouchability is not a short or temporary feature; it is a permanent one. To put it straight, it can be said that the struggle between the Hindus and the Untouchables is a permanent phenomenon. It is eternal, because the religion which has placed you at the lowest level of the society is itself eternal, according to the belief of the Hindu caste people. No change according to time and circumstances is possible. You are at the lowest rung of the ladder today. You shall remain lowest forever. This means the struggle between Hindus and Untouchables shall continue forever. How you will survive through this struggle is the main question. And unless you think over it, there is no way out. Those who desire to live in obedience to the dictates of the Hindus, those who wish to remain their slaves, they do not need to think over this problem. But those who wish to live a life of self-respect and equality will have to think over this. How should we survive through this struggle? For me, it is not difficult to answer this question. Those who have assembled here will have to agree that in any struggle one who holds strength becomes the victor. One who has no strength need not expect success. This has been proven by experience, and I do not need to cite illustrations to prove it.

Three Types of Strength

The question that follows, which you must now consider, is whether you have enough strength to survive through this struggle? Three types of strength are known to man: (i) manpower, (ii) finance and (iii) mental strength. Which of these do you think that you possess? So far as manpower is concerned, it is clear that you are in a minority. In the Mumbai Presidency, the untouchables are only one-eighth of the total population.

Dalit women often take jobs washing clothes

That, too, unorganized. The castes within themselves do not allow them to organize. They are not even compact. They are scattered through the villages. Under these circumstances, this small population is of no use as a fighting force to the untouchables at their critical moments. Financial strength is also just the same. It is an undisputed fact that at least you have a little bit of manpower; but finances you have none. You have no trade, no business, no service, no land. The pieces of bread thrown out by the higher castes are your means of livelihood. You have no food, no clothes. What financial strength can you have? You have no capacity to get redress from the law courts.

Thousands of untouchables tolerate insult, tyranny and oppression at the hands of Hindus without a sigh of complaint because they have no capacity to bear the expenses of the courts. Regarding mental strength, the condition is still worse. The tolerance of insults and tyranny without grudge and complaint has killed the sense of retort and revolt. Confidence, vigor and ambition have been completely vanished from you. All of you

Dalits often have daily construction jobs with extremely low wages

have become helpless, unenergetic and pale. Everywhere, there is an atmosphere of defeatism and pessimism. Even the slight idea that you can do something does not enter your mind.

Muslim Example

If whatever I have described above is correct, then you will have to agree with the conclusion that follows. The conclusion is, if you depend only upon your own strength, you will never be able to face the tyranny of the Hindus. I have no doubt that you are oppressed because you have no strength. It is not that you alone are in the minority. The Muslims are equally small in number. Mahar-Mangs also have only a few houses in the village. But no one dares to trouble the Muslims, while you are always victims of tyranny. Why is this so? Though there may be two Muslim houses in the village, nobody dares to harm them, while the whole village practices tyranny against you though you have ten houses. Why does this happen? This is a very pertinent question and you will have to find a suitable answer. In my opinion, there is only one answer to this question. The Hindus realize that the strength of the whole of the Muslim population in India stands behind those two houses of Muslims living in a village and, therefore, they do not dare to touch them. Those two houses also enjoy a free and fearless life because they are aware that if any Hindu commits aggression against them, the whole Muslim community from Punjab to Madras will rush to their protection at any cost. On the other hand, the Hindus are sure that no one will come to your rescue, nobody will help you, no financial help will reach you. Tahsildar and the police belong to caste Hindus, and in case of disputes between Hindus and Untouchables, they are more faithful to their caste than to their duty. The Hindus practice injustice and tyranny against you only because you are helpless.

Outside Support

From the above discussion, two facts are very clear. First, you can not face tyranny without strength. And second, you do not possess enough strength to face the tyranny. With these two conclusions, a third one automatically follows. That is, the strength required to face this tyranny must be secured from outside. How you gain this strength is really an important question. You will have to think this over with an unbiased mind.

From this, you will realize one thing, that unless you establish close relations with some other society, unless you join some other religion, you cannot get the strength from outside. It clearly means you must leave your present religion and assimilate yourselves with some other society. Without that, you cannot gain the strength of that society. As long as you do not have strength, you and your future generations will have to lead your lives in the same pitiable condition.

Spiritual Aspect of Conversion

Until now, we have discussed why conversion is necessary for material gains. I propose to put forth my thoughts as to why conversion is as much necessary for spiritual well being. What is religion? Why is it necessary? "That which governs people is religion." That is the true definition of religion. There is no place for an individual in Hindu society. The Hindu religion is constituted on a class-concept. Hindu religion does not teach how an individual should behave with another individual. A religion which does not recognize the individual is not personally acceptable to me.

Three factors are required for the uplift of an individual. They are: sympathy, equality and liberty. Can you say by experience that any of these factors exist for you in Hinduism?

No Equality in Hinduism

Such a living example of inequality is not to be found anywhere in the world. Not at anytime in the history of mankind can we find such inequality, which is more intense than untouchability. I think you have been thrust into this condition because you have continued to be Hindus. Those of you who have become Muslims are treated by the Hindus neither as Untouchables nor as unequals. The same can be said of those who have become Christians.

That God is all pervading is a principle of science and not of religion because religion has a direct relation with the behavior of man. Hindus can be ranked among those cruel people whose utterances and acts are two poles apart. They have this Ram on their tongues and a knife under their armpits. They speak like saints but act like butchers.

Thus we are not low in the eyes of the Hindus alone. We are the lowest in the whole of India because of the treatment given to us by the Hindus.

If you have to get rid of this same shameful condition, if you have to cleanse this filth and make use of this precious life, there is only one way. That is to throw off the shackles of the Hindu religion and the Hindu society in which you are bound.

The taste of a thing can be changed; but the poison cannot be made removed. To talk of annihilating caste is like talking of removing the poison. In short, so long as we remain in a religion which teaches a man to treat another man like a leper, the sense of discrimination on account of caste, which is deeply rooted in our minds, can not go. For annihilating caste and untouchability, change of religion is the only antidote.

Untouchables are not Hindus

What is there in conversion which can be called novel?

Really speaking, what sort of social relations have you with the caste Hindus at present? You are as separate from the Hindus as Muslims and Christians are. So is their relation with you. Your society and that of the Hindus are two distinct groups. By conversion, nobody can say or feel that one society has been split. You will remain as separate from the Hindus as you are today. Nothing new will happen on account of this conversion. If this is true, then why should people be afraid of conversion? At least, I do not find any reason for such a fear.

Revolution - Not Reform

Changing a religion is like changing a name. Change of religion followed by the change of name will be more beneficial to you. To call oneself a Muslim, a Christian, a Buddhist or a Sikh is not merely a change of religion, but also a change of name. Since the beginning of this movement of conversion, various people have raised various objections to it. Let us now examine the truth, if any, in such objections.

A congenital idiot alone will say that one has to adhere to one's religion because it is that of one's ancestors. No sane man will accept such a proposition. Those who advocate such an argument seem not to have read the history at all. The ancient Aryan religion was called Vedic religion. It has three distinct characteristics (features): beef-eating, drinking and merry-making. All were part of the religion of the day. Thousands of people followed it in India and even now some people dream of going back to it. If the ancient religion alone is to be adhered to, why did the people of India leave Hinduism and accept Buddhism? Why did they divorce themselves from the Vedic religion? Thus, this Hindu religion is not the religion of our ancestors, but it was a slavery forced upon them.

To reform Hindu society is neither our aim nor our field of action. Our aim is to gain freedom. We have nothing to do with anything else.

If we can gain freedom by conversion, why should we shoulder the responsibility of reforming the Hindu religion? And why should we sacrifice our strength and property for that? None should misunderstand the object of our movement as being Hindu social reform. The object of our movement is to achieve social freedom for the untouchables. It is equally true that this freedom cannot be secured without conversion.

Caste Can't be Destroyed

I do accept that the untouchables need equality as well. To secure equality is also one of our objectives. But nobody can say that this equality can be achieved only by remaining Hindu and not otherwise. There are two ways of achieving equality. One, by remaining in the Hindu fold and another by leaving it by conversion. If equality is to be achieved by remaining in the Hindu fold, mere removal of the sense of being a touchable or an untouchable will not serve the purpose. Equality can be achieved only when inter-caste dinners and marriages take place. This means that the Chaturvarnya must be abolished and the Brahminic religion must be uprooted. Is it possible? And if not, will it be wise to expect equality of treatment by remaining in the Hindu religion? And can you be successful in your efforts to bring equality? Of course not. The path of conversion is far simpler than this. Hindu society does not give equality of treatment, but the same is easily achieved by conversion. If this is true, then why should you not adopt this simple path of conversion?

Conversion is the Simplest Path

According to me, this conversion of religion will bring happiness to both the Untouchables, as well as the Hindus. So long as you remain Hindus, you will struggle for social intercourse, for food and water, and for inter-caste marriages. And so long as this quarrel continues, relations between you

Only Dalits may deal with dead animals

and the Hindus will be of perpetual enemies. By conversion, the roots of all the quarrels will vanish. Thus by conversion, if equality of treatment can be achieved and the affinity between the Hindus and the Untouchables can be brought about, then why should the Untouchables not adopt the simple and happy path of securing equality? Looking at this problem at this angle, it will be obvious that the path of conversion is the only right path of freedom which ultimately leads to equality. It is neither cowardice nor escapism.

Sanctified Racism

Although the castes exist in Muslims and the Christians alike, it would be cruel to liken it to that of the Hindus. There is a great distinction between the caste-system of the Hindus and that of the Muslims and Christians. First, it must be noted that though the castes exist amongst the Christians and the Muslims, it is not the chief characteristic of their social body. There is one more difference between the caste system of the Hindus and that of the Muslims and Christians: the caste system in the Hindus has the foundation of religion. The castes in other religions have no sanction in their religion. Hindus cannot destroy their castes without destroying their religion. Muslims and Christians need not destroy their religions for eradication of their castes. Rather, their religion will support such movements to a great extent.

Conversion Alone Liberates Us

I am simply surprised by the question which some Hindus ask us concerning what can be achieved by conversion alone? Most of the present day Sikhs, Muslims and Christians were formerly Hindus; the majority of them being from the Sudras and Untouchables. Do these critics mean to say that those who left the Hindu fold and embraced Sikhism or Christianity have made no progress at all? If this is not true, and if it is admitted that conversion has brought a distinct improvement in their condition, then to say that the untouchables will not benefit by conversion carries no meaning.

After giving deep thought to the problem, everybody will have to admit that conversion is as necessary to the Untouchables as self-government is to India. The ultimate object of both is the same. There is not the slightest difference in their ultimate goal. The ultimate aim is to attain freedom. If freedom is necessary for the life of mankind, conversion of the Untouchables which brings them complete freedom, cannot be called worthless by any stretch of the imagination.

Economic Progress or Social Change?

I think it necessary here to discuss the question as to what should be initiated first, whether economic progress or conversion? I do not agree with the view that economic progress should precede.

Untouchability is a permanent handicap on your path to progress. Unless you remove it, your path cannot be safe. Without conversion, this hurdle cannot be removed.

So, if you sincerely desire that your qualifications should be valued, your education should be of some use to you, you must throw away the shackles of untouchability, which means that you must change your religion.

However, for those who need this Mahar Watan, I can assure them that their Mahar Watan will not be jeopardized by their conversion. In this regard, the Act of 1850 can be referred. Under the provisions of this Act, no rights of person or his successors with respect to his property are affected by virtue of his conversion.

Pune Pact

A second doubt is about political rights. Some people express fear as to what will happen to our political safeguards if we convert. But I feel it is not proper to depend solely on political rights. These political safeguards are not granted on the condition that they shall be everlasting. They are bound to cease sometime. According to the Communal Award of the British Government, our political safeguards were limited for 20 years. Although no such limitation has been fixed by the Pune Pact, nobody can say that they are everlasting. Those who depend upon political safeguards must think as to what will happen after these safeguards are withdrawn on the day on which our rights cease to exist. We will have to depend on our social strength. I have already told you that this social strength is wanting in us. So also I have proved in the beginning that this strength cannot be achieved without conversion.

Political Rights

Under these circumstances, one must think of what is permanently beneficial.

In my opinion, conversion is the only way to eternal bliss. Nobody should hesitate even if political rights are required to be sacrificed for this purpose. Conversion brings no harm to the political safeguards. I do not understand why the political safeguards should at all be jeopardized by conversion. Wherever you may go, your political rights and safeguards will accompany you. I have no doubt about it.

If you become Muslims, you will get political rights as Muslims. If you become Christians, you will get political rights as Christians. If you become Sikhs, you will have political rights as Sikhs. In short, our political rights will accompany us.

So nobody should be afraid of conversion. On the other hand, if we remain Hindus and do not convert, will our rights be safe? You must think carefully on this. Suppose the Hindus pass a law whereby untouchability is prohibited and its practice is made punishable. Then they may tell you, "We have abolished untouchability by law and you are no longer untouchables."

Looking through this perspective, conversion becomes a path for strengthening political safeguards rather than becoming a hindrance. If you remain Hindus, you are sure to lose your political safeguards. If you want to save them, leave this religion. The political safeguards will be permanent only by conversion.

The Hindu religion does not appeal to my conscience. It does not appeal to my self-respect. However, your conversion will be for material, as well as for spiritual gains. Some people mock and laugh at the idea of conversion for material gains. I do not hesitate in calling such people stupid.

Conversion Brings Happiness

I tell you all very specifically, religion is for man and not man for religion. To get human treatment, convert yourselves.

CONVERT -For getting organized

CONVERT -For becoming strong

CONVERT -For securing equality

CONVERT -For getting liberty

CONVERT -For a happy domestic life

I consider him as leader who without fear or favor tells the people what is good and what is bad for them. It is my duty to tell you what is good for you, even if you don't like it. I must do my duty. And now I have done it.

It is now for you to decide and discharge your responsibility.

Appendix Two
Spiritual Fascism and Civil Society
by Dr. Kancha Ilaiah
Used with Permission

Hinduism and the Right to Religion

Ever since Mr. Vajpayee called for a debate on the "conversions" of the tribals of Gujarat into Christianity, a debate has been taking place on the question of conversion. At the same time, the Hindutva forces were occasionally targeting the missionaries in different parts of the country. The visit of Pope John Paul II and the adoption of the document "Ecclesia in Asia" at the Asian Papal Conference of the Catholic Church have thrown a challenge to the major religions of Asia, namely Buddhism, Hinduism and Islam. One major statement that the document made was: "Just in the first millennium the Cross was planted on the soil of Europe, and in the second on that of America and Africa, we can pray that in the third Christian millennium a harvest of faith will be reaped in the (Asian) continent." Let us not forget the fact that behind this hope of the Church there are many European states whose moral loyalty the Catholic Church commands. If the implications of such commitment of the European populace to the Church as seen in the context of the emergence of the European Union where still Catholicism is the commanding religion as against the Protestant

125

Young Dalit girls often work instead of going to school

dominated U.S., the trend becomes clearer. Very interestingly, the Ecclesia in Asia document appears to present a homogenized view of Christianity by setting aside the internal conflicts between Catholicism and Protestantism. The recent attacks of the Hindutva forces on Indian Christians seem to have helped them to view Christianity as a monolith.

More than in any other nation in Asia, undoubtedly India provides a fertile ground to "reap the harvest of faith" for the Church because of the contesting social pluralities that got built into the Indian system due to the graded unequal caste system. The Hindu clergy, despite the assertion of the Hindutva brigade, did not make it clear whether Hinduism is a religion or a way of life. If the clergy defines it as a religion, it has never shown nor is there any such evidence forthcoming from their on-going practice that like all other universal religions it treads the path of inclusiveness. The exclusionism of the Brahmin clergy is an essential ethical value of the Hindu mode of life. Leave alone the non-existence of a one God, one book ethic for Hinduism – as that had come to be known as a core principle of an inclusionist religion, the basic "right to religion" has not been granted to the Scheduled Tribes, the Scheduled Castes and even to the Sudras who are being characterized as Other Backward Castes in many parts of the country after the Constitution recognized such a social category. Apart from the claims of Hindu political leaders like Mahatma Gandhi during the freedom struggle and proclamation of the leaders of the Hindutva forces, there is no policy statement of the top Hindu clergy declaring that the non-dwijas are part of Hinduism. A major chunk of the non-dwija population constitutes the STs, SCs and OBCs

If we take the top modern interpreters of Hinduism – Gandhiji, S. Radhakrishnan and P.V. Kane – only Gandhiji characterized Hinduism as a religion and hence asked for the adoption of inclusionism as its policy and also everyday practice because a religion invariably must be inclusivist. Radhakrishnan and Kane defined Hinduism basically as a way of life. Once it is defined as a way of life with a huge divide of civil society into two broad camps called dwijas and Sudras – Chandalas with a distinct divide of food habits, modes of cooking, worship and so on, which way of life could be characterized as Hindu? Assuming that the dwija way of life is characterized as Hindu, does not that automatically suggest that the non-dwija way of life is outside the framework of Hinduism? In all religions the priestly class constructs boundaries for people's way of life, and the practices that the priests uphold become the central way of life of the people who belong to that religion. This is where the religion has its own belongingness. If Hinduism is a way of life wherein the boundaries of that way of life are either not defined or the cultural life process of the people not homogenized with a principle of cultural equality, it cannot claim the authority of a religion over the people at all. The rights of such people, who are outside the cultural boundaries of the priesthood, to embrace any other religion which provides them the social and cultural advantages of that religion must be respected. Here the concept "conversion" cannot be invoked.

If the Brahmin clergy declare that Hinduism is a religion like any other it is their spiritual duty to grant all the people the right to become priests and interpret its tenets based on their life experience.

In this modern democratic phase of Indian society two things become central for the exercise of the right religion: One the right to priesthood and second the right to communicate with the divine in one's own mother tongue. These two are mutually interlinked rights in a society where historically language was used as an instrument of spiritual suppression. In other words, if the Brahmin clergy of India declare that the SCs, the STs and the OBCs are Hindus, their right to priesthood and their right to use all non-Sanskritic languages as ritually correct language must also be recognized. But unfortunately till today there is tremendous resistance to giving theological training to children coming from all castes and there is more resistance to allowing languages other than Sanskrit for prayer. Resisting the reform of Hinduism and not allowing the right to embrace any other religion by characterizing it as "conversion" as the Hindutva forces do today amounts to asking the vast majority of the people to remain in "religious darkness." This is nothing but religious fascism. It is important to note that Christianity allows the right to priesthood and the right to use the mother-tongue as lingua franca as a matter of spiritual pragmatism. The Christian religion in India granted these basic rights to whoever embraces it, though it could not eradicate the caste system within.

Do the Sudras and Chandalas in the classical sense or the SCs, STs and OBCs in the modern sense have the right to choose any religion and embrace it in the absence of a universal declaration by the Hindu clergy? Do the Hindu clergy or the Hindutva forces who do not even talk about reform in Hinduism as much as the Arya Samaj or Gandhiji talked about it have the right to ask the people of India not to embrace any other religion? Can the Prime Minister who came from the caste of Hindu clergy declare his agenda of reform? Do the dwijas who practice a life of "difference" have a right to tell the Christian clergy not to assimilate the SCs, STs and OBCs into a universally recognizable religion? The concept of religious conversion is linked to the fact that one is already within one religion and when he/she changes his/her religion; that becomes a conversion. But what the tribals in Gujarat or Orissa were doing was embracing Christianity but not converting into it. What right have the dwijas, who see themselves as different, to define embracing of any religion by the non-dwijas, who also consider themselves as different, as conversion? If dwijahood is rebirth, according to Hindu religion, at least all SCs, STs and all Sudras should have been given that dwijahood a long time ago.

Whether it is the Prime Minister or the organized brigade of the Hindutva Parivar, they have no moral authority to use an inclusivist language to defend an exclusivist religion. Either they will have to fight for reforms within Hinduism whereby its present structure completely changes or they will have to allow the masses to look for avenues available outside it. With the mere fact that the state machinery is at their command they cannot bulldoze the ignorant masses.

Religion And Democracy

The discourse on the question of the individual and the community (or caste) rights of religion in relation to Hinduism must also be viewed from the point of view of strengthening democracy in India. It is a known fact that religion is a civil societal system and democracy is a political system. Some of the recent political theoreticians, of course, divided democracy to non-political spheres, particularly to the sphere of civil society. But the relationship between religion and democracy always remained a dark area in theoretical discourses.

In the day to day life of the individual and with caste, religion and democracy reinforcing each other, they also operate antithetically de-legitimizing each other. For example, in a country such as ours, even in the absence of the right to religion for several caste communities in civil society, in the political sphere they could get the right to vote after we adopted constitutional democracy. If civil society closes some important options to individuals, the right to vote in the political sphere does not make the individual a fully matured democratic being. Only when all options in civil society open to all, does a personality that can make use of political rights evolve.

In Hindu civil society, the options before its youth in choosing their direction in life – spiritual, secular or political – is closed to all except Brahmin youth. For all others, the right to choose a spiritual profession is closed. For Dalit-Bahujans, Hindu religion does not even give an initiation. In the universally known non-Hindu religious civil societies such as Christianity, Islam or Buddhism, all youth (at least male youth – the gender discrimination must be noted) are given religious initiation. They can choose to become a Jesuit, a Mullah or a Monk, or they can choose a secular profession such as medicine or engineering. Or they can choose to become political leaders. But for all Sudra

(OBC), SC and ST youth, the option to pursue the spiritual line of life is closed. Thus, a major section of Indian youth in the present religious relationship cannot enter into a religious profession at all. Though this is basically a civil societal right, its absence impinges upon the formation of the personality of the individual and this has implications for democracy. Who is responsible for this situation? What solution does the RSS have for this problem? How does Mr. Atal Behari Vajpayee who became the first Prime Minister from a Hindu religious ideological party resolve this contradiction?

The 70-80 years of work of the RSS did not do anything to resolve this contradiction. It did not address the basic question of untouchability, leave alone the right to religion. It worked very hard to politicize Hinduism but never to democratize it. After the BJP came to power, it is sending a large number of RSS cadre to tribal areas to spread Hinduism. Do all those tribals who are taken into Hinduism get dwijahood or equal rights within that religion? What is the mode of initiation they undergo

Families of Dalits work together doing back-breaking labor

to call themselves Hindus? Can they call themselves Hindus by retaining their historical food culture which includes beef as well? Within Hinduism in which caste will they be located? Do the tribals embrace Christianity or Islam because these religions offer that scope making all food and linguistic cultures inclusive? Vegetarianism for the Shankaracharyas or for that matter for any Brahmin priest, for example, is not a question of a personal habit but a religious condition. In this mode of religious conditioning how does the tribal essence of life (food, drink and so on) fit in?

The attempts of the RSS to communalize the Sudras and SCs by constructing the enemy image of Muslims and Christians did not make them Hindus with all the religious rights that other universal religions offered. With the present understanding of religion, the RSS is not going to make the STs, SCs, and OBCs Hindus with mere declarations. It has failed to construct Hinduism as a religion of love and brother/sisterhood. The RSS did not expand the civil societal space to Sudras, SCs and there is no indication that it would expand that for the tribals either. Expansion of such space is based on opening of the spiritual line of promotion to people who are said to be part of such religious society. Neither Golwalker's writings nor those of Vivekananda show any way out for this contradiction in Hinduism. But this question remains central for its survival – leave alone expansion.

The right to choose a spiritual line of life and to reach the top position in that line is part of the larger civil societal democratic rights of every individual. This issue acquires a political, democratic significance when some individuals or communities are said (or claimed) to be part of that religion but denied that right. When the civil societal right to be equal with all its members is denied, the State and the judicial institutions have the right to intervene.

This is where the Indian State and judiciary have failed all these years. The Indian judiciary while examining questions relating to Hinduism must keep this inequality in mind. The judiciary must also remember that without having the foundation of "social democracy" at the base level, political democracy will remain fragile. This was the point that Ambedkar stressed much before he embraced Buddhism. Surprisingly, the Hindu priests, politicians and judges seem to think even now that religious inequality and political inequality can exist side by side. Such inequalities do not co-exist. Any amount of suppression of Dalit-Bahujans within the Sangh Parivar (as happened in the case of Kalyan Singh) or outside, while winking at the real problem is not going to stop the structural fragmentation of civil society. Christianity or Islam provide to those who want a civil societal democracy in day-to-day life an equalitarian identity different from anything Hinduism can think of in the near future. This is where the crisis of Hinduism lies and this is going to haunt it in the 21st Century.

In the western context Christian religious relationship and civil and political democratic relationship have evolved as historical social mishmash. Once the church emerged as an institution the serf and the feudal lord got equal rights to worship and to become members of one spiritual civil society. This, however, did not give them equal political rights. These were given as capitalism and democracy evolved hand-in-hand.

Hindu religion strangely right from its inception negated that elemental spiritual democracy. In the Bhakti movement some Sudras found the right to worship Hindu deities with great reluctance, that too in the face of the major threat from Islam, the right to worship was granted to only Sudras. But this was not a great change. It was just one step from the Ramayana period when Shambhuka lost his life only for asking for the right to ownership. Until today, Hindu organizations, including the RSS, have not altered the religious position of the Sudras. The situation of the SCs is worse.

In the modern period two people tried to reform Hinduism from two different ends – from above Gandhi and from below Ambedkar. Gandhi not only failed to democratize it but to the shock of the world was killed by the Hindutva fanatics themselves. Ambedkar attempted to reform it for a long time. Having realized that it was impossible to reform it he embraced Buddhism just before his death. Nehru must have thought that modernization of India would automatically reform Hinduism too. But his agenda too failed. Even today Hindu civil society stands in contradiction with the democratic

Dalits must labor in the most difficult of climates

essence of human society. What is the solution of the RSS to this fundamental problem? If the RSS and the Brahmin clergy do not understand this historical contradiction, Indian democracy will collapse more irretrievably than that of Pakistan. Do they want that to happen?

Spiritual Fascism and Civil Society

Whenever I raise the question of the socio-cultural negation of the Hindu religion, there are many who take serious objection to such a discourse. Do they think that there is absolutely no need for reform in that religion? If they think that reform is not required, how do they change the hierarchy-ridden system which suffers from inequalities, poverty and destitution? If they think that reform is necessary, what sort of reform do they think is possible? The Rastriya Swayam Sevak Sangh and its allied organizations have been trying to unite the so-called Hindus without talking a word about the caste system. Some Hindu thinkers blamed the British. They claimed that the British policy of "divide and rule" created caste in this country. Some thinkers go to the extent of saying that the British were responsible for every social divide including caste and communal politics. Many of these are from Hindu orthodox and fundamentalist groups. They are out to do enormous damage to the Indian nation. Needless to say, most of these theoreticians are Brahmins. This method of constructing history is a conspiracy against Dalit-Bahujans. The Brahmins succeeded in their aim because most Dalit-Bahujans were denied education. The Brahmins invoked religion to keep them illiterate. The Brahminical forces were extremely unhappy when the Britishers made education available to the Dalit-Bahujans. As a consequence, the educated among the Sudra, Chandala, Adivasis, (SCAs) including those who work within the Sangh

Parivar, were led into thinking that they would get equal rights within the present Hindu framework. But they were mistaken.

Those who have been defending the present structure of Hindu civil society have a responsibility to take on the challenge. Can they spell out their program of reform? Do they believe in abolition of caste or not? In the process of moving towards abolition of caste, is it or is it not essential to work towards the equalization of social status of castes? Will the Madigas, Malas, Mangalis, and Chakalis enjoy the same social status as Brahmins? How do the RSS and the BJP intend to bring about equal status between all castes? What are their specific programs? Do the people of this country have a right to know their mind as a ruling party or not? With religious power, political power and social power being in their hands, can't they initiate reform? If they cannot, why do they talk about Hindu unity?

The famous Brahmin historian D.D. Kosambi said that it was at the insistence of Kautilya that the Brahmin priests were delegated the task of dividing tribals into castes and in the process subdue the Sudras and Chandalas. At that point in history, the only social forces that were challenging the Kautilyan State were the tribals. The Brahmins used two instruments: the karma theory and candneeli to thwart any revolt. Further, their division into caste was an ancient method of Hinduization. Hinduization, thus, was used as a mode to establish structural divisions. At what state were the Sudras divided into several castes is not exactly known. Ever since the divine theory of varna was constructed the socio-political direction of the Hindu thinkers was to divide the social groups into non-unifiable social units which gradually became castes. Never in its history of three millennia were the thinkers who made an attempt to unite them to form a broader positive religion allowed to succeed in their attempt.

In the twentieth century, the major attempt to unite such divided groups from below was started by Ambedkar and from above by Gandhi, Gandhi being a Vaisya with a non-dwija Jain background, tried to combine the Jain mode of ahimsa and the Christian mode of passive resistance. It is a known fact that Gandhi borrowed the concept of passive resistance from Henry David Thoreau. In other words, for Gandhi Vardhamana Mahaveer and Thoreau's Civil Disobedience were the main ideals. But Gandhi was a clever tactician. Since he had led the Congress party that consisted mainly of Hindu fundamentalist Brahmins, he was using the Bhagawad Gita and the names of Rama and Krishna only as a tactical move. Otherwise, how would the concept of ahimsa and Rama, Krishna, and Gita go together? It was his aim to establish Hindu unity without dismantling the caste system. Even that was not tolerated by the Brahminical forces of India. Christopher Jaffrelot – in his well researched book *The Nationalist Movement and Indian Politics* – says, "Gandhi was resented by high caste Hindus because he posed a real danger to their social position. His mobilization of the lower strata of society threatened to alter the basic characteristics of Indian society by making its cultural periphery its center. Here lay one of the main reasons why Nathuram Godse decided to kill Gandhi. This Chitpavan Brahmin felt all the more insecure because his socio-economic status was very precarious whereas Maratha and Gujarati Baniyas were emerging as the new upwardly mobile groups of Maharastra. The himsavada ideology of Brahmanism reached its peak with the murder of Gandhi."

However, Ambedkar saw a serious limitation in Gandhian ideology. Gandhi, on the other hand, saw a danger to Hindu unity in Ambedkar's liberative reservation program. As a result, the compromised Pune Pact came into being. The Brahmins within the RSS did not approve of the agreement between Gandhi and Ambedkar as they did not want any emancipation of Dalits to take place. This was where the Chitpavan Brahmins of Maharashtra planned a way to eliminate him and they did so. A protagonist of non-violence was eliminated violently. Ambedkar, on the other hand, proposed his annihilation of caste theory based on the Buddhist and Rousseau's theories of liberty, equality and fraternity. He waited until the end of his life. He finally realized that Hinduism was beyond reform and embraced Buddhism. This is the historical background of intolerance towards social reform in India. In other words, the Hindu ideology was rooted in the concept of "divide and rule" and on the "hegemonization of the other". The main reason for the stagnation of Hinduism is rooted in its "spiritual fascism". Not many have realized that spiritual fascism in the civil society and political democracy do not go hand in hand for long.

Once spiritual fascism was established by the Brahmin thinkers, neither the 800-year rule of Muslim kings, nor the 200-year rule of the mighty British empire could break that caste system, which was the main instrument of divide and rule. The roots of caste system lie in "spiritual fascism". The basis of spiritual fascism is the belief: "I am superior to the other." The concept of aham Brhmasmi in Hinduism is based on the concept of exclusivism. It also assigns the role of God to one's own self. The Brahmin self-declared itself as Godhood and always stood against production of food from the soil. That is the reason why all Hindu heroes proclaim that they themselves are Gods. They do not even consider themselves agents of God/Goddess. In contrast, all other religions survive on prophethood.

Despite their status as untouchable, Dalits often perform services that benefit the entire community.

One does not find humility in Hindu assertions at all. This ideology of human beings declaring themselves as God has strong tendency of spiritual fascism. The Hindu exclusivism is constructed around this spiritual fascism that institutionalizes itself within the ideological sphere of spiritualism. The SCs, STs, and OBCs are victims of this spiritual fascism. One of the main characteristics of spiritual fascism is that in this mode anybody can directly declare himself as God. Spiritual fascism, however, does not give much scope for women to be equals with men in any sphere.

The caste system killed the basic initiative among people even to embrace other organized equalitarian religions. The terrorization of Dalit-Bahujans by using brutal violence was so complete that Hegel said in his famous book *The History of Philosophy* that the Indian masses lost their soul and spirit in this violent division of the society. Spiritual fascism ensures that the people of the country cannot form themselves into a nation. A nation is not a political entity. "It is a philosophical, economic, civilizational, cultural and spiritual entity. Men and women from all walks of life must play an equal role in all the spheres mentioned above.

The Sangh Parivar as a Brahminical organization, cannot build this nation as a globally respectable civilized nation because it has no agenda for human equality. Its agenda of Hindu unity does not address the question of human equality. How do their theoreticians think that the Sudras, Chandalas and Adivasis (SCAs) even know when they are getting educated, without having the right to occupy the highest position in the spiritual domain and by leaving it to Brahmin (caste) will keep quiet and serve the interests of spiritual fascists even in this century and millennium? The radical reform I have been talking about is to weed out the spiritual fascism that got institutionalized in our civil society. Naturally, those who benefited from such spiritual fascism defend it from various points of view. But the fundamental question is that those who lost the essence of life need to be liberated from such spiritual fascism.

When nation states began to institutionalize themselves, as Hegel pointed out, the human being first sought the integration of the spirit. A civil society which upholds spiritual hierarchization imposes all kinds of restrictions on human development. The Indian State remains totally disintegrated because of the anti-people ideology of Brahminism. Brahminism has to deconstruct itself if it wants a peaceful transformation of Indian society, by integrating itself with the whole of Sudra, Chandala and Adivasi food, pooja and production culture. If Hinduism wants to reconstruct itself, as the teams of Brahmin pandits went into Adivasis at the instance of Kautilya to divide them into castes, let them now go to Adivasi, SC and OBC wadas to integrate them by eating their food, by sleeping in their houses, by giving up the cultural isolationism and exclusivism of Brahmanism. The protagonists of Hinduism must accept this challenge.

Where Should the Reform Begin

Where do we begin the reform in our society? With untouchability, of course. When we say this, everyone, including a Brahmin, a Reddy, or an OBC pretends to agree. But the question is how to go about it? Reform has to begin from the core of the system. It should start with a change in the thinking of all social forces involved. Reform should start from where such practice began.

P.V. Kane, father of modern Brahminism, who has been awarded Bharat Ratna for re-writing Dharmasatra, says, "Untouchability did not and does not arise by birth alone. It arises in various ways. In the first place, persons become outcaste and untouchable by being guilty of certain acts that amount to grave sins. For example, Manu prescribes that those who are guilty of Brahmin murder, theft of Brahmana's gold or drinkers of liquors should be excommunicated, no one should dine with them or teach them, or officiate as priests for them, nor should marriage relationship be entered with them."

But what we see around is that children born in the 59 SC castes in Andhra Pradesh alone, before they could walk and talk, leave alone involve in any sinful activity, abusing or

Dalits are highly-skilled laborers, experts in their crafts

involving in theft or murdering any Brahmin by the very definition of Kane – become untouchables. Is there no solution to this? Yes. There is a solution.

If we go by the investigations into our socio-economic and cultural life, the contribution of these castes has been far greater than any other caste. If we go by that cumulative contribution, all those who live as untouchables today must be accorded the highest status. The status of the caste communities has been defined in terms of their relationship with the Hindu priests. The Hindu priesthood is linked up, apart from caste, to the Sanskrit language. Look at the diabolism of the Indian nationalism. If one takes the caste statistics, the highest number of children studying in schools established by Christian missionaries in the English medium are Brahmins. Leading theoreticians who condemn missionary education and others who eulogize Sanskrit as the prime national language again come from the same caste. Those whom the very same theoreticians condemn as unethical and un-nationalistic – the Dalit-Bahujans – are forced to study the mother-tongue centered languages like Telugu, Hindi, Kannada, Bengali and so on. In fact, what is good for a Brahmin should also be good for the other castes and without being hypocritical they should have declared English as our national language. Like the vast majority of Brahmins and the rich belonging to other castes, for children of the poor who study in government schools English should be taught as a primary language. And every child's mother-tongue should be taught as the second language. Then there would be no hypocrisy.

The issue of rooting out untouchability is even now linked to the question of popular priesthood. The Indian state must acquire control over all the temple activities and appoint untouchables and none else (at least for a few decades) as priests. They should also serve as ritual priests in the households of all caste communities.

Here again the question of language arises. The Brahminical argument is that the mantra pattana (chanting of mantras) in temples and in the rituals should take place only in Sanskrit. Where are so many SCs who know Sanskrit? The answer to the problem is simple. In the relationship between God and the people, it is the content of the discourse of communication that matters, not the language. The State, therefore, should make arrangements for translation of the mantras from Sanskrit to Telugu (for example in Andhra Pradesh) and the mantras pattana both in the temples and in other rituals can take place in Telugu (already taking place in Tamil), Hindi, Kannada, Marathi and for that matter in English also if people want it. The priests would say that such talk, leave alone the action, is blasphemous. What is actually blasphemous is their own practice, not the attempt to reform.

A major dissection of the relationship between the language spirituality and social control should take place. The modern democratic state cannot and should not close its eyes to this fundamental aspect of social transformation. Even spiritually it is unethical to say you can communicate with Gods/ Goddesses in only this language and not in others. Look at the politics of priesthood. Their presumption of the Aryan Hindu gods understanding Sanskrit and hence reciting of a Sanskrit mantra is understandable. But how can they presume that a Goddess like Pochamma (to propitiate whom they recite Sanskrit mantras) would also understand a Sanskrit shloka? How can the priests presume that Shiridi Saibaba, a son of a boat-man/ woman who talked to people in Marathi wanted a mantra to be recited in Sanskrit?

The construction of God/Goddess images in a particular language is a political construction to retain the hegemony of the priestly class. The universal assumption is that gods and goddesses can be prayed to in any language and within the sphere of the old prayers they can be translated into all other languages and new prayer can be written in any language that the bhakta of that God/Goddess can communicate in.

The State must stop this politics of language in the sphere of religion. Prayer in any religion should take place in any language. The people have a right to communicate with any God/Goddess they believe in, in their own language. If a particular religion claims that a particular community is a part of that religion, it should automatically grant it the right to priesthood. In any organization, the right to reach the highest position is central to the organization – whether it is spiritual, political or economic.

Since Hinduism is claiming that Scheduled Castes, Scheduled Tribes and OBCs are part of it, the right to priesthood must be given to them by the State.

M.N. Srinivas a Brahmin sociologist who proposed the theory of Sanskritization of the society says, "A priest is a representative of the religion and the theological system which commanded the respect and allegiance of all, including the political head on religious occasions." A radical change in this institution and its body and language is called for. For 4,000 years, the Dalit-Bahujans of India were denied the power of priesthood.

For not allowing them all these years, the Shankaracharyas of all peethas should apologize to the SCs, STs and OBCs. The SCs must be given a ceremonial apology in all temples of India for being kept untouchable. If the priestly class does not do that it has no right to tell the people not to embrace Christianity or any other religion that wants to give them that right to priesthood and the power to control religious institutions. That amounts to preserving religious fascism through electoral politics.

Shifting of priesthood to Dalit-Bahujans along with changing of the language and discourse between the bhakta and the God/Goddess in India amounts to the beginning of Dalitization of the spiritual system. Unlike the numerically small Brahmin caste, no Dalit-Bahujan caste as a whole can turn into a priestly caste. While one person holds the position of priest, the other will be an agrarian worker, another will be tanner in the same family and another one may, perhaps, hold a government job.

Thus, one family will operate as a unit of multi-cultural and economic skills. The productivity, creativity and spirituality operate in a language of communicability in the family, community (then not caste) and also the village. If an untouchable becomes the priest, who can command respect in every house he should not recreate the culture of paada pooja of the priest. He should be a democratic representative of the spiritual agency who talks your language, who drinks your water and eats your cooked food. A democratic relationship between priest, people and God/Goddess changes the structure of temples where, as Phule says, "Plundering and property making" from temple money would stop; where temples may become simple and small with murthy (idol) or without a murthy.

Dalits are given jobs no upper caste person would want

For neatly bathed and dressed students and teachers, like in convent schools, the temples serve the purpose of schooling during the day, while morning and evening prayers can take place. Thus, every village can have a temple and a school as well.

Chandrababu Naidu must realize that this reform of translating and doing mantra pattana in Telugu in all the temples in Andhra Pradesh and appointing Dalit-Bahujans as priests is a must even for the socio-economic modernization that he is talking about. Otherwise, the Telugu nationality will not acquire the self respect that he is talking about. Secondly, unless the priesthood is shifted into the untouchable community, the social status of untouchables at the village level will not change.

Without undertaking this reform, organizing any number of Janma Bhoomis, or constituting any number of judicial commissions like that of the Justice Pannaiah Commission will not solve the problem. A respectable political party that conducted a survey in Andhra Pradesh discovered about 25 forms of untouchability being practiced in every district.

If this reform is not taken up by the State in deference to the argument of the priests, India will shamelessly be carrying untouchability and Brahminical casteism into the 21st century wherein the angry untouchables shall tear the Indian system apart. Let us not allow that to happen.

Appendix Three

The U.S. Should Stop Caste Virus
by Udit Raj
Used with Permission

America is really a melting pot of various ethnic traditions, cultures and civilizations. India claims this, too, but caste has not allowed it to truly happen. The address of a person, his physical appearance, and his qualifications do not complete the identity of a Hindu until he discloses his caste lineage. India houses its stock of population from Eurasia, Europe and Asia through migration at different intervals. However, most of them still maintain their identity more than as fellow brothers and countrymen. Needless to mention that most of the US population is from Spain, England, Denmark, France and other parts of Europe. In less than 300 years these migrants have become more American than their ancestors were. People who migrated to America in recent decades have become Americans first. Dr. Rochinga Pudaite based in Colorado Springs, running Bibles for the World, is proud to say, "We Americans", although he migrated from India about 40 years ago. Almost all places of the world have contributed and still contribute their population to the USA and they eventually melt together into one people. This is contrary to India. The Aryans came to India about 3,000 years ago, but still have not melted with the aborigines.

Any society or country can afford foreign wrath or the worst type of calamity. However, no country can handle internal conflicts for sustained time as has been evidenced in India. This has given birth to undeclared civil war. For about 3,000 years and before Independence, India could not win a single battle. Whoever attacked or invaded, was successful without much resistance. Two to three hundred Afghanis and Middle Eastern aliens had hardly any hindrance in reaching Delhi. The simple reason was the division of Indians among the four castes: Brahmins on the top of the hierarchy who were supposed to be born from the mouth of God; Kshatriyas occupying the second slot were born from the arms of God who were assigned to defend the boundary of the country from invaders and establish law and order; Vaishyas, falling in the third strata of society, were meant to carry out trade and commerce, their origin of birth from stomach of God; and at the bottom were Sudras (Dalits) who were to do menial and scavenging work, their origin attributed to the feet of God.

The quality of the Indian soil and climate is excellent; but the social system does not allow the translation of the fruits of modern democracy, technology and education. British imperialism left behind many institutions like the judiciary, bureaucracy and the parliamentary system. To run a parliamentary or democratic form of government, political parties are a must. People know that political parties are in the background managing the largest democracy in the world, but essentially it is the social system which is more effective in this role. Competition among political parties are between castes rather than ideologies or the articulation of special interest groups. Germany and other countries are having elections on issues like the environment and the unification of Europe. However, our democracy has not evolved beyond basic needs

Dalits are victims of physical, emotional and spiritual oppression

like housing, clothing and education. Poverty is justified under the garb of simplicity, spiritualism and immaterialism.

Caste Hindus can give up anything including their own life. However, they can never shed their caste attitude. In 1998 when I was invited to attend the first Dalit International Convention in Kuala Lumpur, Malaysia, it was originally unbelievable to me. About 150 years ago, the British took the Indians to Malaysia as laborers and assistants. Eventually Indians made their home there. More than one million Hindus live in Malaysia, and they still maintain their caste identity. Dalits living in Malaysia have many grievances which followed them from India. So far, no medicine has been created to kill the caste virus. However, Lord Buddha effectively created a counter revolution to demolish caste. All Buddhist temples and other remnants were destroyed and we are learning through the accounts of Chinese travelers and other sources that there was once a great Buddhist religion.

Recently, two taxi drivers of Indian origin in in Vancouver, Canada, had an argument. The upper caste driver assaulted and uttered casteist remarks against the Dalit driver and later made an appeal to the management to suspend the Dalit driver. How can North America escape the caste menace?

Hundreds of thousands of Hindus are quickly settling in San Francisco, Dallas, and other parts of the US. Are Americans aware of the caste virus which is spreading through them in their own American society? No doubt Hindus are very intelligent and hard working and are doing well in engineering, information technology and medicine. But at what cost? In early July 2004, I was visiting San Francisco when my host took me sightseeing. He informed me that the Hindu community follows caste and religious rituals including Kumbh Mela - a festival during which Hindus come together to perform religious rites, even in America. In fact, these rituals and customs are the sources of the caste system and discrimination. Is the American government aware of these social activities which will disrupt the American social equilibrium in the future?

The UN Conference on race, caste and related intolerance in Durban, South Africa, in 2001, sensitized the world to the victimization of the Dalits. As a natural corollary, so called upper castes faced and are going to face questions on social discrimination. But their simple and clinching answer is generally, "It is our way of life." Every wrong and social discrimination is justified in the name of Hindu culture. But, when it comes to the liberation of the Blacks in South Africa, these caste Hindus would be in forefront asking for restoration of human dignity and rights. Murder, rape, torture of the Dalits (and Bahujans, Sudras, Other Backward Castes) are the order of the day. If anyone questions these actions, the simple reply will be that it is the Hindu way of life.

The US attack on Iraq is a subject of great concern, but injustice and the worst form of discrimination against their own brethren, the Dalits, is not important. This emanates from the philosophy that Dalits are not human beings. When five Dalits were lynched for the carcass of a so-called holy cow in Jhajjar, Haryana, in 2002, this heinous act was supported by a statement of the Vice President of the Vishwa Hindu Parishad that as per Hindu structure, the life of a cow is more important than the life of a Dalit.

Economic globalization is being welcomed in India, but what about cultural globalization? Indian businessmen are fascinated with American businesses, working culture, product quality and service efficiency, but when it comes to bearing their social obligation, they change their tune. Affirmative action for African-Americans and Hispanics no longer fascinates them.

Recently the Indian Congress-led government has once again regained power at the Center. They promise to give jobs to Dalits in the private sector. However, this promise met with big opposition from business houses. Media, business, film, export and import, education, modern technology and other important fields are controlled by the upper castes. They oppose anything which empowers marginalized people. Newborn abandoned Dalit children can be eaten by dogs and animals, but if a Christian missionary gives the same child shelter in an orphanage, the RSS - an outfit of Hindu fundamentalists - will

Dalits are coming together to break free from caste bondage

attack the missionary saying he is forcibly converting the child. In Hindu society, if any child is abandoned it is because of his sins in a past life and therefore he should suffer. The mother of such child is a criminal because she gave birth to the child outside of marriage. An unwanted female child is also cast aside because women have an inferior position in Hindu society.

About two years ago, the Vishwa Hindu Parishad (VHP) had a rally in America in order to encourage orthodox Hinduism among secular Hindus living in America. Americans did not object. Hindu priests are not denied American visas on the grounds that they will propagate Hinduism. But Christian missionaries are denied Indian visas. Why are Hindus afraid? The US may be proud of synthesizing everyone coming in to the country, but will have serious problems in the future because of the caste virus. If about 250 million lower castes have suffered in India because of caste discrimination, all human beings are duty-bound to help others avoid inhuman treatment. Nothing is greater than humanity, be it sovereignty of the country or the community interest.

I wish that my fellow brothers in America will not spread this virus. I, being Dalit, do not mean that I don't love Hindus living in the US. I simply love humanity more.

Appendix Four
November 4, 2001 Analysis
by Dr. Joseph D'souza

At the end of the day it seemed that the event of November 4 played to a divine script. The anticipated violence did not take place. The Dalits once again displayed their tremendous peaceful and good nature. There were no untoward incidents. No one tried to aggravate an already very tense and difficult situation. Nevertheless several things happened that are of serious concern.

There was a blatant suppression of democratic rights. For all its efforts and propaganda to create a positive image in international circles (especially in the USA where it raises a lot of finances) and media, the BJP/Sangh Parivar used all the powers of the State to brutally suppress and restrict the gathering of Dalits. The Delhi police who are under the Home Ministry have a lot to answer for in revoking the permissions at the last minute and then blocking the entry of Dalits at all major road entry points into Delhi. One had to just ask any Dalit who managed to get in to the Ambedkar Bhavan about the difficulties they had to cross to come to the premises.

The collusion of the National Commission on Minorities, the Delhi police and the VHP was in full evidence. Christian leaders are simply amazed how the machinery of the State crushes the Dalits. If the State could blatantly do it in the capital city of Delhi, what on earth is going on in the villages and towns?

There was a tremendous showing of true grit. The broken people demonstrated that they were made of steel as they gathered together in defiance of the ban and going ahead with the conversions in a makeshift arrangement literally done at the last hour. Tens of thousands of Dalits flowed to the Ambedkar Bhavan (despite all the official attempts to prevent them) to reject the caste system and the Hindu Social Order that imposed this inhuman social and spiritual system on them for over 3,000 years. The amazing thing about the crowds was the sheer number of women that turned up for the conversion ceremony.

All through the day, Ram Raj was heard calling different police officers to release his people at the outskirts of Delhi who were being prevented from coming in. Trains, buses and trucks were not allowed to bring in the people. A disinformation campaign was launched in the morning saying that only 3,000 people had gathered at the venue. Another disinformation campaign was that the conversion event was cancelled.

However, the national and international media were there to see the tens of thousands within and outside the venue (on the roads) who were participating in the conversion ceremony. It is difficult to assess the correct figure of how many people came to the venue throughout the day. Figures vary. BBC quoted 60,000. Jain TV quoted 100,000. The disinformation brigade said 3,000-8,000. As an overall figure for the day right up to the evening when Dalits were still coming, it would be safe to say that approximately 100,000 people came to the venue throughout the day and joined in for the conversions. Added to that, as one Hindi paper reported, more people were prevented from entering into Delhi than those who finally managed to get in even as late as midnight on November 4 itself.

Ram Raj became Udit Raj. For those of us who were guests on the dais, the conversion ceremony was a revelation. The symbolism of it was powerful. First a Dalit Indian Buddhist monk shaved the head of Ram Raj and administered the oaths. Brahmins can only perform such religious rites according to the caste system. Next, a series of vows were read out and agreed to. Ambedkar developed some of them. In the vows was the rejection of the gods that had failed the Dalits and the system that had oppressed them. A series of vows revolved around a moral code.

The Dalits who had names of gods announced the change of their names. "Ram" was dropped and he took on the name "Udit" meaning "arisen". To the utter jubilation of the crowd, the Buddhist monk presented "Udit Raj" to the crowd. Then Udit Raj led the crowds in the repetition of vows and the

Dalits are thrilled to be part of the Quit Hinduism movement

conversion ceremony with a monk presiding over the function. This mass conversion will have a major impact on the nation, even in the future.

Udit Raj made a significant speech. The main speech had a few major themes: the rejection of Hinduism and the caste system; the oppression of the Sangh Parivar and the BJP; a political stance towards those who had not given open support to the movement; and for the first time in many, many decades the Christian Church was defended openly from a public platform in the glare of international media and the right of the Dalits to embrace Christianity.

This represents a major breakaway from past events and also from Indian politics' accusations that the Christian Church and the Christian West was bent upon converting Indians. Udit Raj also called the bluff of the upper castes who themselves freely associate with Christian English education and queue up to migrate to the West, but at the same time eagerly denounce them at home. This was against the backdrop of the VHP accusation that this event was a Christian conspiracy. There was huge applause for this process of spiritual friendship between Christians and Dalits:

There was a major Christian presence and participation on that day. Many hundreds of Christian leaders from India and observers from the West were present to witness the event and express solidarity with the Dalits as they sought liberation. Three Christian leaders were given the opportunity to speak and the following themes emerged: 1) Christians were there as invitees and guests to the Dalit function (this was not, as some wide publicity had announced, a Christian convention); 2) Christians were there to support the Dalits' freedom of conscience and choice to choose their own destiny in the face of increasing oppression; 3) The Indian Church expressed public support for the Dalits' right to choose; 4) The Dalit-Christian solidarity declared in Hyderabad earlier in 2001 would continue solidly in the days ahead; and 5) Christians were there because Jesus loved the Dalits and Christians were committed to bringing that love of Jesus to the Dalits in word and in deed.

No doubt, there was Christian activity surrounding that event. Christians were wise during the event. Some Christians provided food packets, but most of all there was simply interaction and brotherhood as human beings. Christian love was demonstrated in whatever way possible. Christians followed the directions given by the Dalit leaders since it was their event. Christian courage was in full display because each one there knew that they could end up being targets of the VHP and the State.

I think that the Church's open stand with the Dalits and their movement for liberation has put the Indian Church at the right side of history. The Indian Church is part and parcel of the struggle of the Dalits and the Backward castes. Needless to say, the Body of Christ has the opportunity to demonstrate the full love of Jesus, from Calvary to the touching and healing of the leper, to millions of people who will be warm to them.

The Dalit cry for empowerment through quality Christian English-based education has to be heard by the worldwide Church. Otherwise, our love for them is going to look very hollow. Jesus has given us education as the weapon of the weak. It liberates them here and now.

Caste-based churches in India who for so long have been able to get away with enforcing the caste system in the Church. They will have to confront this new reality. Some hard soul searching is needed in the present context. The Dalit-Bahujan communities will not be silent and quiet anymore. They will be fierce in their criticism against the Church wherever they find caste discrimination.

Broader alliance with Indian civil society on basic human rights issues will need to increase in the days to come. We have seen with our own eyes in Delhi how the powers of the State can be used to crush the expression of freedom of conscience. The VHP believes in only one kind of religious freedom – join them or get out of the way.

Appendix Five
Biography of Mahatma Phule
by Dr.Y.D. Phadke
From the book, Slavery, by Mahatma Phule; Used with Permission

This brief Life Sketch of Mahatma Jotirao Phule is written by the noted scholar Dr. Y.D. Phadke. He is the editor of the Collected Words of Mahatma Phule in Marathi. He is also an eminent scholar of Mahatma Phule and the Satyashodhak Movement.

JOTIRAO GOVINDRAO PHULE occupies a unique position among the social reformers of Maharashtra in the nineteenth century. While other reformers concentrated more on reforming the social institutions of family and marriage, with special emphasis on the status and right of women, Jotirao Phule revolted against the unjust caste system under which millions of people had suffered for centuries. In particular, he courageously upheld the cause of the untouchables and took up the cause of the poorer peasants. He was a militant advocate of their rights. The story of his stormy life is an inspiring saga of a continuous struggle which he waged relentlessly against the forces of reaction. Though some keen observers of the social scene in Maharashtra like Narayan Mahadeo Parmananda did acknowledge his greatness in his lifetime, it is only in recent decades that there is increasing appreciation of his service and sacrifice in uplifting the masses.

163

Jotirao Phule was born in 1827. His father, Govindrao, was a vegetable-vendor in Pune. Originally Jotirao's family were known as Gorhays and came from Katgun, a village in the Satara district of Maharashtra. His grandfather, Shetiba Gorhay, settled down in Pune. Since Jotirao's father and two uncles served as florists under the last of the Peshwas, they came to be known as 'Phule'. Jotirao's mother passed away when he was just one year old. After completing his primary education, Jotirao had to leave the school and help his father by working on the family's farm. Jotirao's marriage was celebrated when he was not even thirteen.

Impressed by Jotirao's intelligence and his love of knowledge, two of his neighbors, one a Muslim teachr and the other a Christian gentleman, persuaded Jotirao's father to allow Jotirao to study in a secondary school. In 1841, was admitted to the Scottish Mission's High School at Pune. It was in this school that he met Sadashiv Ballal Govande, a Brahmin, who remained a close friend throughout his life. Both Jotirao and Govande were greatly influenced by Thomas Paine's ideas and they read with great interest Paine's famous book *The Rights of Man*. Moro Vithal Valvekar and Sakharam Yashwant Paranjapye were two other Brahmin friends of Jotirao who in later years stood by him in all his activities. After completing his secondary education in 1847, Jotirao decided not to accept a job with the Government.

An incident in 1848 made him aware of the iniquities of the caste system; specifically, the predominant position of the Brahmin in the social setup. He was invited to attend a wedding of one of his Brahmin friends. As the bridegroom was taken in a procession, Jotirao accompanied him along with the relatives of his Brahmin friends. Knowing that Jotirao belonged to a caste considered to inferior by the Brahmins, the relatives of the bridegroom insulted and abused him. Jotirao left the procession

Mahatma Phule stood for the rights of both Dalits and women

and retuned home. With tears in his eyes, he narrated his experience to his father who tried to pacify him. After this incident, Jotirao made up his mind to defy the caste system and serve the Sudras and women who were deprived of all their rights as human beings under the caste system.

Education of women and the lower castes, he believed, deserved priority. Hence, he began educating his wife Savitribai and opened a girls' school in August 1848. The orthodox opponents of Jotirao were furious. They started a vicious campaign against him. He refused to be unnerved by their malicious propaganda. As no teacher dared to work in a school in which untouchable children were admitted as students, Jotirao asked his wife to teach the girls in his school. Stones and brickbats were thrown at her when she was on her way to the school. The reactionaries threatened Jotirao's father with dire consequences if he did not dissociate himself. Yielding to the pressure, Jotirao's father asked his son and daughter in-law to leave his house as both of them refused to give up their noble endeavor.

Though the school had to be closed for sometime due to lack of funds, Jotirao re-opened it with the help of his Brahmin friends Govande and Valvekar. On July 3, 1851, he founded a girls' school in which eight girls were admitted on the first day. Steadily the number of student increased. Savitribai taught in this school and had to suffer a lot because of the hostility of the orthodox people. Jotirao opened two more girls' schools in 1851-52. In a memorial addressed to the Education Commission (popularly known as the Hunter Commission) in 1882, he described his activities in the field of education, "A year after the institution of the female school, I also established an indigenous mixed school for the lower classes, especially the Mahars and Mangs. Two more schools for these classes were subsequently added. I continued to work in them for nearly nine or ten years."

Jotirao was aware that primary education among the masses in the Bombay Presidency was very much neglected. He argued that "a good deal of their poverty, their want of self-reliance, their entire dependence upon the learned and intelligent classes" could be attributed to the British government for spending a profusely large portion of revenue on the education of the higher classes. According to him, this policy resulted in the virtual monopoly of all the higher offices under the government by the Brahmins.

Jotirao boldly attacked the stranglehold of the Brahmins, who prevented others from having access to avenues of knowledge and influence. He denounced them as cheats and hypocrites. He asked the masses to resist the tyranny of the Brahmins. All his writings were variations on this theme. His critics made fun of his ignorance of grammar and philology, his inelegant language, and his far-fetched interpretation of Indian history and the ancient texts. They brushed his criticism aside by saying that he was merely echoing what the Christian missionaries had said about Indian society in general and Brahmins in particular. The established scholars of his time did not take Phule's arguments seriously. His critics did not realise that Jotirao's acrimonious criticism was basically a spontaneous outburst of a genuine concern for the equal rights of human beings. Emotionally he was so deeply involved in his work that he could not make a dispassionate analysis and take a detached view of the social forces. Jotirao's deep sense of commitment to basic human values made it difficult for him to restrain himself when he witnessed injustice and atrocities committed in the name of religion by those who were supposed to be its custodians.

Widow remarriages were banned and child-marriage was very common among the Brahmins and other upper castes in the then Hindu society. Many widows were young and not all of them could live in a manner in which the orthodox people expected them to live. Some of the delinquent widows resorted to abortion or left their illegitimate children to die on the streets. Out of pity for the orphans, Jotirao Phule established an orphanage, possibly the first such institution founded by a Hindu. Jotirao gave protection to pregnant widows and assured them that the orphanage would take care of their children. It was in this orphanage run by Jotirao that a Brahmin widow gave birth to a boy in 1873 and Jotirao adopted him as his son.

For sometime, Jotirao worked as a contractor for the government and supplied building materials required for the construction of a huge barrage at Khadakvasala near Pune. He had the experience of working with the officials of the Public

Because of oppression, Dalit women are forced to make difficult choices with regard to their own well being and the well being of their children

Works Department which was notoriously corrupt. The clerks and other officers were invariably Brahmin and they exploited the illiterate workers. Jotirao felt it necessary to explain to the workers how they were duped by the Brahmin officials. In one of the ballads Jotirao composed, he described vividly the fraudulent practices resorted to by the Brahmin officials in the Public Works Department.

In 1868, Jotirao decided to give access to the untouchables to a small bathing tank near his house. In his controversial book called Slavery published in June 1873, Jotirao included a manifesto which declared that he was willing to dine with anyone, regardless of their caste, creed or country of origin. It is significant that several newspapers refused to give publicity to the manifesto because of its contents. His book Slavery was severely criticised for its "venomous propaganda" against the Brahmins. Jotirao dedicated this book "to the good people of the United States as a token of admiration for their sublime, disinterested and self-sacrificing devotion in the cause of Negro Slavery". The book is written in the form of a dialogue. After tracing the history of Brahmin domination in India, Jotirao examines the motives and objects of cruel and inhuman laws framed by the Brahmins. Their main object in fabricating these falsehoods was to dupe the minds of the ignorant and rivet firmly the chains of perpetual bondage and slavery which their selfishness and cunning had forged. The severity of the laws affecting the Sudras and the intense hatred with which they were regarded by the Brahmins can be explained on no other supposition but that there was originally between the two a deadly feud arising from the advent of the latter into this land. Jotirao argued that the Sudras were the sons of the soil, while the Brahmins came from outside and usurped everything that was possessed by the "not one hundredth part of the rogueries" that were generally practsed on his "poor, illiterate and ignorant Sudra brethren".

On September 24, 1873, Jotirao convened a meeting of his followers and admirers and it was decided to form the 'Satya Shodhak Samaj' (Society of Seekers of Truth) with Jotirao as its first president and treasurer. Every member had to take a pledge of loyalty to the British Empire. The main objectives of the organization were to liberate the Sudras and Ati Sudras and to prevent their exploitation by the Brahmins. All the members of the Satya Shodhak Samaj were expected to treat all human beings as children of God and worship the Creator without the help of any mediator. Membership was open to all and the available evidence proves that some Jews were admitted as members.

In 1876, Jotirao refused to regard the Vedas as sacrosanct. He opposed idolatry and denounced the chaturvarnya. In his book *Sarvajanik Satya Dharma Pustak* published in 1891, his views on religious and social issues are given in the form of dialogue. According to him, both men and women were entitled to enjoy equal rights and it was a sin to discriminate between human beings on the basis of sex. He stressed the unity of man and envisaged a society based on liberty, equality and fraternity. He was aware that religious bigotry and aggressive nationalism destroy the unity of man.

In 1876 Jotirao was nominated as a member of the Pune Municipality. He tried to help the people in the famine-stricken areas of Maharashtra when a severe famine in 1877 forced people in the rural areas to leave their villages. Some of them had to leave their children behind. An appeal issued on May 17, 1877 by Jotirao indicates that the Victoria Orphanage was founded under the auspices of the Satya Shodhak Samaj to look after these unfortunate children. From the beginning of the year 1879, Krishnarao Bhalekar, one of Jotirao's colleagues, edited a weekly called "Deenbandhu" which was the organ of the Satya Shodhak Samaj. The weekly articulated the grievances of the peasants and workers. "Deenbandhu" defended Jotirao when Vishnushastri Chiplunkar, a powerful spokesmen of the conservative nationalists, attacked Jotirao's writing in the most vitriolic style.

Narayan Meghaji Lokhande was another prominent colleague of Jotirao. Lokhande is acclaimed as the Father of the Trade Union Movement in India. From 1880 onward, he looked after the management of "Deenbabdhu" which was published from Bombay. Along with Lokhande, Jotirao also addressed the meetings of the textile workers in Bombay. It is significant that his colleagues Bhalekar and Lokhande had previously tried to organize the peasants and the workers, but no such attempt had been made by any organization to redress their grievances.

One of the charges leveled by Jotirao against the leaders of the Brahmo Samaj, the Prarthana Samaj, the Sarvajanik Sabha and the Indian National Congress was that despite their programs, in reality, they did very little to improve the lot of the masses. He felt that these organizations were dominated by the Brahmins and were not truly representative in character. In his booklet called "Satsara" (The Essence of Truth) published in June 1885, he criticized the Brahmo Samaj and the Prarthana Samaj. Addressing their leaders he declared, "We don't need the help of your organizations. Don't worry about us." In his book, *Sarvajanik Sabha or the Indian National Congress,* he warned that the persistent demand made by these organizations for Indianization of the administrative services, if accepted, would lead to Brahminization of the service in India. He thought that it was difficult to create a sense of nationality so long as the restriction on dining and marrying outside of caste continued to be observed by people belonging to different castes. Education of the masses would promote the process of nation-making.

It should be remembered that just as Jotirao did not mince words when he criticized the leaders of the movements he was equally fearless in criticizing the decisions of the alien rulers which did not contribute to the welfare of the masses. When the government wanted to grant more licenses for liquor shops, Jotirao condemned this move as he believed that addiction to liquor would ruin many poor families. On November 30, 1880, the President of the Pune Municipality requested the members to approve his proposal of spending 1,000 Rupees on the occasion of the visit of Lord Lytton, the Governor-General of India. The official wanted to present him an address during his visit to Pune. Lytton had passed an Act which resulted in gagging the press and "Deenbandhu", the organ of the Satya Shodhak Samaj, protested against the restriction on the right to freedom of the press. Jotirao did not like the idea of spending the money of the taxpayers in honoring a guest like Lytton. He boldly suggested that the amount could be very well spent on the education of poor people in Pune. He was the only member out of all the 32 nominated members of the Pune Municipality who voted against the official resolution.

Another incident also revealed his attachment for the poor peasants and his courage in drawing the attention of members of the British royal family to the suffering of the farmers in rural areas. On March 2, 1888, Hari Raoji Chiplunkar, a friend of Jotirao, arranged a function in honor of the Duke and Duchess of Connaught. Dressed like a peasant, Jotirao attended the function and made a speech. He commented on the rich invitees who displayed their wealth by wearing diamond studded jewelery and warned the visiting dignitaries that the people who had gathered there did not represent India. If the

Dalits wait patiently for their chance at human dignity

Duke of Connaught was really interested in finding out the condition of the Indian subjects of Her Majesty the Queen of England, Jotirao suggested that they ought to visit some nearby villages, as well as the areas in the city occupied by the untouchables. He requested the Duke of Connaught who was a grandson of Queen Victoria to convey his message to her and made a strong plea to provide education to the poor. Jotirao's speech created quit a stir.

Throughout his life. Jotirao Phule fought for the emancipation of the downtrodden people. The struggle which he launched at a young age ended only when he died. He was a pioneer in many fields and among his contemporaries he stands out as one who never wavered in his quest for trust and justice. Though he was often accused of fomenting hatred among the non-Brahmins, very rarely was an attempt made to consider his scathing criticism in a broad perspective. The later generation also took considerable time to understand and appreciate the profound significance of his unflinching espousal of the rights of man. This remained until the end of his life a major theme of his writings and a goal of his actions.

Appendix Six
Cow and Culture
by Dr. Kancha Ilaiah
Used with Permission

They killed five Dalits for skinning a cow... At least now the whole nation must stand up against this kind of spiritual and political nationalism.

Is a cow's life worthier than that of five Dalits? The Dalits have had to pay an enormous price — for remaining untouchables — for removing carcasses from villages and towns for thousands of years. They had to pay the price of remaining illiterate and insecure for building up the leather economy of India. If they had not removed dead cattle, dogs and even humans, the people in the towns and villages would have died of disease — dreadful contagious diseases at that. Even now they keep paying a price — sometimes with their lives as happened at Jhajhar in Haryana.

What was essentially scientific was constructed as spiritually bad and sinful in Manudharma Shastra. Such superstitions keep getting passed off as spiritual and scriptural. More shocking is that Hindutva organizations such as the VHP want to implement them, emboldened by the fact that their ideological twins are at the helm of the state. They killed five

The labor of Dalits has dignity

Dalits for skinning a dead cow on a roadside in Haryana. They say the Hindu scriptures prohibit such an act. To bolster their case, for the modernist legal context, the murderers say the Dalit youth were skinning a live cow.

The leather industry was one of the first that Indian society had established, much before the Europeans and Americans. Instead of being proud of them, society rendered the builders "untouchable". There is some thing basically wrong with this mode of understanding divinity and spirituality. The problem is deeper than present behavior of the VHP and its ilk shows. An anti-scientific temper runs deep in the Hindu psyche. Does this not deserve much more serious debate? Is the struggle against such a spiritual psyche to be carried only by the Dalits?

Many of the VHP leaders themselves are industrialists. Some of them are training their children in America — their dreamland — to become successful industrialists. Some of them are even involved in the leather industry. How does the leather industry exist without skinning dead cattle? If doing leather business is not sinful, how does skinning a carcass become sinful? How does leather come into existence without skinning dead animals? The Shastras say that it was for doing this early industrial job that the Dalits became untouchable. Now Dalits get lynched for doing this job. What kind of nationalism is this?

Incidentally, when this took place I had been touring America — the dreamland of many Indians. I met many boys and girls — many of them Brahmin, too — who were working in beef-packing and leather units. A majority of them eat beef as well. Do all of them become untouchables? By invoking the same scriptures that the Hindutva forces are talking about, they too should be declared untouchable and never should be allowed to enter the Hindurashtra that Bal Thackeray is talking about. But these beef-eating NRIs fill their hundis with dollars and hence they are most lovable. How do they explain this mode of Hinduism?

Indians do not live with one mode of scriptures. We have the Buddhist scriptures, and we have had the Bible as a living book for 2,000 years in India. The Quran has been India for more than 1,000 years. The Dalits in the spiritual realm have more affinity with Buddhism and Christianity than Hinduism. In their spiritual realm, the cow is not sacred. How can Hindutva forces impose their spirituality on others? Second, how can spirituality allow so much hypocrisy, terrorism and brutality in day-to-day life? The Hindutva forces want to welcome economic globalization but do not want to learn any thing from the process of cultural globalization. How do the global spiritual cultures see the relationship between animals and human beings? Is it not important to learn from all positive cultures?

In the economic realm, they want to do the leather business. In the political realm, they want to use Dalits as vote givers. In the spiritual realm, the science and technological process that the Dalits as historical people constructed became impure, polluted. Not that the professions in which the OBCs are involved in day-to-day life - washing clothes, making pots and rearing sheep and cattle — have become spiritually acceptable for Hindutva forces. They, too, still — perhaps forever — remain impure. All the Sudras/OBCs involved in productive activity continue to be disallowed from becoming priests in Hindu temples. But their muscle power becomes acceptable to kill Dalits in the name of cow protection, Muslims in the name of religion. Even the Yadavs who work within Hindutva organizations do not ask why the buffalo, that gives us most of our milk, is not sacred.

Our intellectual class does not ask why Hindu nationalism gets constructed around issues such as animal sacredness and human pollution. When I asked this question at Columbia University, the Indian diaspora intellectuals appeared to entirely agree with me. But how much writing they did on such issues is the moot question. What kind of theoretical and practical nationalism do we have? No one asks why the cow alone should remain a constitutionally protected animal under the Directive Principles of State Policy.

Today the whole world knows that the black people's culture has not only been assimilated into American civil society;

it has become part of the state system as well. The American Constitution values black life as absolutely equal to white life. The Indian intellectuals must realize that the civil war, to grant equal rights for blacks, was not fought by blacks. It was fought by whites under the leadership of Abraham Lincoln. African-American taxi drivers tell a lot of positive stories about white intellectuals. They say such things because many whites sacrificed their lives for the freedom of the blacks. Where is such a rebellion against the barbarity of treating the life of a cow as more worthy than that of five Dalits in India? Imagine such a thing taking place against African-Americans today. Would not such an incident have created conditions for another civil war? Look at the way the Indian legal agencies are dealing with this brutality. They are waiting to find out whether the cow was dead or alive when it was skinned.

The Hindutva forces do not think of abandoning such superstitious notions of life and religion. So far there is no evidence of the Hindu spiritual leadership coming down heavily on the VHP leadership even on this issue. The rulers in New Delhi remain indifferent as well. After the BJP came to power, the cow question was brought to the national agenda again and again. Earlier, it was always in reference to Muslims. Now Dalits get lynched. Their very livelihood is attacked.

The OBCs who are getting used in all kinds of fundamentalist activities, including the Gujarat pogrom, possibly must have been used in this lynching of Dalits as well. Many Dalit activists have been complaining that the OBCs are getting involved in attacks against them more and more. The OBCs must realize that the very same fundamentalists are going to say that the caste hierarchical practices must come into operation in classical form. They may disqualify them to contest elections and administer the state. The Hindutva attacks did not stop with

Muslims. They targeted Christians and now the Dalits. At least now the whole nation must stand up against this kind of spiritual and political nationalism.

Appendix Seven
Annihilation of Caste
by Dr. B.R. Ambedkar
Used with Permission

Speech prepared for the 1936 Annual Conference
of the Jat-Pat-Todak Mandal of Lahore
BUT NOT DELIVERED

*Owing to the cancellation of the Conference by the Reception
Committee on the ground that the views expressed in the Speech
would be unbearable to the Conference*

Friends,

I am really sorry for the members of the Jat-Pat-Todak Mandal
who have so very kindly invited me to preside over this
Conference. I am sure they will be asked many questions for
having selected me as the President. The Mandal will be asked
to explain as to why it has imported a man from Bombay to
preside over a function which is held in Lahore. I believe the
Mandal could easily have found some one better qualified than
myself to preside on the occasion. I have criticised the Hindus. I
have questioned the authority of the Mahatma whom they
revere. They hate me. To them I am a snake in their garden. The
Mandal will no doubt be asked by the politically-minded Hindus
to explain why it has called me to fill this place of honor. It is an
act of great daring. I shall not be surprised if some political Hindus
regard it as an insult. This selection of mine cannot certainly

181

please the ordinary religiously-minded Hindus. The Mandal may be asked to explain why it has disobeyed the *Shastric* injunction in selecting the President. Accoding to the *Shastras*, the Brahmin is appointed to be the Guru for the three *Varnas, varnanam bramhano garu*, is a direction of the *Shastras*. The Mandal therefore knows from whom a Hindu should take his lessons and from whom he should nòt. The *Shastras* do not permit a Hindu to accept any one as his Guru merely because he is well versed. This is made very clear by Ramdas, a Brahmin saint from Maharashtra, who is alleged to have inspired Shivaji to establish a Hindu Raj. In his *Dasbodh,* a socio-politico-religious treatise in Marathi verse *Ramdas* asks, addressing the Hindus, can we accept an Antyaja to be our Guru because he is a Pandit *(i.e. learned)* and gives an answer in the negative. What replies to give to these questions is a matter which I must leave to the Mandal. The Mandal knows best the reasons which led it to travel to Bombay to select a president, to fix upon a man so repugnant to the Hindus and to descend so low in the scale as to select an Antyaja — an untouchable — to address an audience of the *Savarnas.* As for myself you will allow me to say that I have accepted the invitation much against my will and also against the will of many of my fellow untouchables. I know that the Hindus are sick of me. I know that I am not a *persona grata* with them. Knowing all this I have deliberately kept myself away from them. I have no desire to inflict myself upon them. I have been giving expression to my views from my own platform. This has already caused a great deal of heartburning and irritation. I have no desire to ascend the platform of the Hindus to do within their sight what I have been doing within their hearing. If I am here it is because of your choice and not because of my wish. Yours is a cause of social reform. That cause has always made an appeal to me and it is because of this that I felt

I ought not to refuse an opportunity of helping the cause especially when you think that I can help it. Whether what I am going to say today will help you in any way to solve the problem you are grappling with is for you to judge. All I hope to do is to place before you my views on the problem.

II

The path of social reform like the path to heaven at any rate in India, is strewn with many difficulties. Social reform in India has few friends and many critics. The critics fall into two distinct classes. One class consists of political reformers and the other of the socialists.

It was at one time recognized that without social efficiency no permanent progress in the other fields of activity was possible, that owing to mischief wrought by the evil customs, Hindu Society was not in a state of efficiency and that ceaseless efforts must be made to eradicate these evils. It was due to the recognition of this fact that the birth of the National Congress was accompanied by the foundation of the Social Conference. While the Congress was concerned with defining the weak points in the political organisation of the country, the Social Conference was engaged in removing the weak points in the social organisation of the Hindu Society. For some time the Congress and the Conference worked as two wings of one common activity and they held their annual sessions in the same pandal. But soon the two wings developed into two parties, a Political Reform Party and a Social Reform Party, between whom there raged a fierce controversy. The Political Reform Party supported the National Congress and Social Reform Party supported the Social Conference. The two bodies thus became two hostile camps. The point at issue was whether social reform should precede political reform. For a decade the forces were evenly balanced and the battle was fought without victory to either side. It was however evident that the fortunes of the; Social Conference were ebbing fast. The gentlemen who presided over the sessions of the Social Conference lamented that the majority of the educated Hindus were for political advancement and indifferent to social reform and that while the number of those who attended the Congress was very large and the number who did not attend but who sympathized with it even larger, the number of those who attended the Social Conference was very much smaller. This indifference, this thinning of its ranks was soon followed by active hostility from the politicians. Under the leadership of the late Mr. Tilak, the courtesy with which the Congress allowed the Social Conference the use of its pandal was withdrawn and the spirit of enmity went to such a pitch that when the Social Conference desired to erect its own pandal a threat to burn the pandal was held out by its opponents. Thus in course of time the party in favour of political reform won and the Social Conference vanished and was forgotten. The speech, delivered by Mr. W. C. Bonnerji in 1892 at Allahabad as President of the eighth session of the Congress, sounds like a funeral oration at the death of the Social Conference and is so typical of the Congress attitude that I venture to quote from it the following extract. Mr. Bonnerji said :

"I for one have no patience with those who saw we shall not be fit for political reform until we reform our social system. I fail to see any connection between the two. . .Are we not fit (for political reform) because our widows remain unmarried and our girls are given in marriage earlier than in other countries? because our wives and daughters do not drive about with us visiting our friends? because we do not send our daughters to Oxford and Cambridge ?" (Cheers)'

I have stated the case for political reform as put by Mr. Bonnerji. There were many who are happy that the victory went to the Congress. But those who believe in the importance of social reform may ask, is the argument such as that of Mr. Bonnerji final? Does it prove that the victory went to those who were in the right? Does it prove conclusively that social reform has no bearing on political reform? It will help us to understand the matter if I state the other side of the case. I will draw upon the treatment of the untouchables for my facts.

Under the rule of the Peshwas in the Maratha country the untouchable was not allowed to use the public streets if a Hindu was coming along lest he should pollute the Hindu by his shadow. The untouchable was required to have a black thread either on his wrist or in his neck as a sign or a mark to prevent the Hindus from getting themselves polluted by his touch through mistake. In Poona, the capital of the Peshwa, the untouchable was required to carry, strung from his waist, a broom to sweep away from behind the dust he treaded on lest a Hindu walking on the same should be polluted. In Poona, the untouchable was required to carry an earthen pot, hung in his neck wherever he went, for holding his spit lest his spit falling on earth should pollute a Hindu who might unknowingly happen to tread on it. Let me take more recent facts. The tyranny practised by the Hindus upon the Balais, an untouchable community in Central India, will serve my purpose. You will find a report of this in the *Times of India* of 4th January 1928. "The correspondent of the *Times of India* reported that high caste Hindus, viz. Kalotas, Rajputs and Brahmins including the Patels and Patwaris of villages of Kanaria, Bicholi-Hafsi, Bicholi-Mardana and of about 15 other villages in the Indore djistrict (of the Indore State) informed the Balais of their respective villages that if they wished to live among them they must conform to the following rules :

(1) Balais must not wear gold-lace-bordered pugrees.

(2) They must not wear dhotis with coloured or fancy borders.

(3) They must convey intimation of the death of any Hindu to relatives of the deceased—no matter how far away these relatives may be living.

(4) In all Hindu marriages, Balais must play music before the processions and during the marriage.

(5) Balai women must not wear gold or silver ornaments; they must not wear fancy gowns or jackets.

(6) Balai women must attend all cases of confinement of Hindu women.

(7) Balais must render services without demanding remuneration and must accept whatever a Hindu is pleased to give.

(8) If the Balais do not agree to abide by these terms they must clear out of the villages. The Balais refused to comply; and the Hindu element proceeded against them. Balais were not allowed to get water from the village wells; they were not allowed to let go their cattle to graze. Balais were prohibited from passing through land owned by a Hindu, so that if the field of a Balai was surrounded by fields owned by Hindus, the Balai could have no access to his own field. The Hindus also let their cattle graze down the fields of Balais. The Balais submitted petitions to the Darbar against these persecutions; but as they could get no timely relief, and the oppression continued, hundreds of Balais with their wives and children were obliged to abandon their homes in which their ancestors lived for generations and to migrate to adjoining States, viz. to villages in Dhar, Dewas, Bagli, Bhopal, Gwalior and other States. What happened to them in their new homes may for the present be left out of our consideration. The incident at Kavitha in Gujarat happened only last year. The Hindus of Kavitha ordered the untouchables not to insist upon sending their

children to the common village school maintained by Government. What sufferings the untouchables of Kavitha had to undergo for daring to exercise a civic right against the wishes of the Hindus is too well known to need detailed description. Another instance occurred in the village of Zanu in the Ahmedabad district of Gujarat. In November 1935 some untouchable women of well-to-do families started fetching water in metal pots. The Hindus looked upon the use of metal pots by untouchables as an affront to their dignity and assaulted the untouchable women for their impudence. A most recent event is reported from the village Chakwara in Jaipur State. It seems from the reports that have appeared in the newspapers that an untouchable of Chakwara who had returned from a pilgrimage had arranged to give a dinner to his fellow untouchables of the village as an act of religious piety. The host desired to treat the guests to a sumptuous meal and the items served included *ghee* (butter) also. But while the assembly of untouchables was engaged in partaking of the food, the Hindus in their hundred, armed with lathis, rushed to the scene, despoiled the food and belaboured the untouchables who left the food they were served with and ran away for their lives. And why was this murderous assault committed on defenceless untouchables? The reason given is that the untouchable host was impudent enough to serve ghee and his untouchable guests were foolish enough to taste it. Ghee is undoubtedly a luxury for the rich. But no one would think that consumption of ghee was a mark of high social status. The Hindus of Chakwara thought otherwise and in righteous indignation avenged themselves for the wrong done to them by the untouchables, who insulted them by treating ghee as an item of their food which they ought to have known could not be theirs, consistently with the dignity of the Hindus. This means that an untouchable must not use ghee even if he can afford to buy it, since it is an act of arrogance towards the Hindus. This happened on or about the 1st of April 1936 !

Having stated the facts, let me now state the case for social reform. In doing this, I will follow Mr. Bonnerji, as nearly as I can and ask the political-minded Hindus " Are you fit for political power even though you do not allow a large class of your own countrymen like the untouchables to use public school? Are you fit for political power even though you do not allow them the use of public wells? Are you fit for political power even though you do not allow them the use of public streets? Are you fit for political power even though you do not allow them to wear what apparel or ornaments they like? Are you fit for political power even though you do not allow them to eat any food they like? " I can ask a string of such questions. But these will suffice, I wonder what would have been the reply of Mr. Bonnerji. I am sure no sensible man will have the courage to give an affirmative answer. Every Congressman who repeats the dogma of Mill that one country is not fit to rule another country must admit that one class is not fit to rule another class.

How is it then that the Social Reform Party last the battle? To understand this correctly it is necessary, to take note of the kind of social reform which the reformers were agitating for. In this connection it is necessary to make a distinction between social reform in the sense of the reform of the Hindu Family and social reform in the sense of the reorganization and reconstruction of the Hindu Society. The former has relation to widow remarriage, child marriage etc., while the latter relates to the abolition of the Caste System. The Social Conference was a body which mainly concerned itself with the reform of the high caste Hindu Family. It consisted mostly of enlightened high caste Hindus who *did* not feel the necessity for agitating for the abolition of caste or had not the courage to agitate for it. They felt quite naturally a greater urge to remove such evils as enforced widowhood, child marriages etc., evils which prevailed among them and which were personally felt by them. They did not stand up for the reform of the Hindu society. The battle that was fought centered round the question of the reform of the family. It did not relate to the social reform in the sense of the break-up of the caste system. It was never put in issue by the reformers. That is the reason why the Social Reform Party lost.

I am aware that this argument cannot alter the fact that political reform did in fact gain precedence over social reform. But the argument has this much value if not more. It explains why social reformers lost the battle. It also helps us to understand how limited was the victory which the Political Reform Party obtained over the Social Reform Party and that the view that social reform need not precede political reform is a view which may stand only when by social reform is meant the reform of the family. That political reform cannot with impunity take precedence over social reform in the sense of reconstruction of society is a thesis which, I am sure, cannot be controverted. That the makers of political constitutions must take account of social forces is a fact which is recognized by no less a person than Ferdinand Lassalle, the friend and co-worker of Karl Marx. In addressing a Prussian audience in 1862 Lassalle said :

" The constitutional questions are in the first instance not questions of right but questions of might. The actual constitution of a country has its existence only in the actual condition of force which exists in the country: hence political constitutions have value and permanence only when they accurately express those conditions of forces which exist in practice within a society"

But it is not necessary to go to Prussia. There is evidence at home. What is the significance of the Communal Award with its allocation of political power in defined proportions to diverse classes and communities? In my view, its significance lies in this that political constitution must take note of social organisation It shows that the politicians who denied that the social problem in India had any bearing on the political problem were forced to reckon with the social problem in devising the constitution. The Communal Award is so to say the nemesis following upon the indifference and neglect of social reform. It is a victory for the Social Reform Party which shows that though defeated they were in the right in insisting upon the importance of social reform. Many, I know, will not accept this finding. The view is current, and it is pleasant to believe in it, that the Communal Award is unnatural and that it is the result of an unholy alliance between the minorities and the bureaucracy. I do not wish to rely on the Communal Award as a piece of evidence to support my contention if it is said that it is not good evidence. Let us turn to Ireland. What does the history of Irish Home Rule show? It is well-known that in the course of the negotiations between the representatives of Ulster and Southern Ireland, Mr. Redmond, the representative of Southern Ireland, in order to bring Ulster in a Home Rule Constitution common to the whole of Ireland said to the representatives of Ulster: " Ask any political safeguards you like and you shall have them." What was the reply that Ulstermen gave? Their reply was " Damn your safeguards, we don't want to be ruled by you on any terms." People who blame the minorities in India ought to consider what would have happened to the political aspirations of the majority if the minorities had taken the attitude which Ulster took. Judged by the attitude of Ulster to Irish Home Rule, is it noting that the minorities agreed to be ruled by the majority which has not shown much sense of statesmanship, provided some safeguards were devised for them? But this is only incidental. The main question is why did Ulster take this attitude? The only answer I can give is that there was a social problem between Ulster and Southern Ireland the problem between Catholics and Protestants, essentially a problem of Caste. That Home Rule in Ireland would be Rome Rule was the way in which the Ulstermen had framed their answer. But that is only another way of stating that it was the social problem of Caste between the Catholics and Protestants, which prevented the solution of the political problem. This evidence again is sure to be challenged. It will be urged that here too the hand of the Imperialist was at work. But my resources are not exhausted. I will give evidence from the History of Rome. Here no one can say that any evil genius was at work. Any one who has studied the History of Rome will know that the Republican Constitution of Rome bore marks having strong resemblance to the Communal Award. When the kingship in Rome was abolished, the Kingly power or the *Imperium* was divided between the Consuls and the Pontifex Maximus. In the Consuls was vested the secular authority of the King, while the latter took over the religious authority of King. This Republican Constitution had provided that, of the two Consuls one was to be Patrician and the other Plebian. The same constitution had also provided that, of the Priests under the Pontifex Maximus, half were to be Plebians and the other half Patricians. Why is it that the Republican Constitution of Rome had these provisions which, as I said, resemble so strongly the provisions of the Communal Award? The only answer one can get is that the Constitution of Republican Rome had to take account of the social division between the Patricians and the

Plebians, who formed two distinct castes. To sum up, let political reformers turn to any direction they like, they will find that in the making of a constitution, they cannot ignore the problem arising out of the prevailing social order.

The illustrations which I have taken in support of the proposition that social and religious problems have a bearing on political constitutions seem to be too particular. Perhaps they are. But it should not be supposed that the bearing of the one on the other is limited. On the other hand one can say that generally speaking History bears out the proposition that political revolutions have always been preceded by social and religious revolutions.

The religious Reformation started by Luther was the precursor of the political emancipation of the European people. In England Puritanism led to the establishment of political liberty. Puritanism founded the new world. It was Puritanism which won the war of American Independence and Puritanism was a religious movement. The same is true of the Muslim Empire. Before the Arabs became a political power they had undergone a thorough religious revolution started by the Prophet Mohammad. Even Indian History supports the same conclusion. The political revolution led by Chandragupta was preceded by the religious and social revolution of Buddha. The political revolution led by Shivaji was preceded by the religious and social reform brought about by the saints of Maharashtra. The political revolution of the Sikhs was preceded by the religious and social revolution led by Guru Nanak. It is unnecessary to add more illustrations. These will suffice to show that the emancipation of the mind and the soul is a necessary preliminary for the political expansion of the people.

III

Let me now turn to the Socialists. Can the Socialists ignore the problem arising out of the social order? The Socialists of India following their fellows in Europe are seeking to apply the economic interpretation of history to the facts of India. They propound that man is an economic creature, that his activities and aspirations are bound by economic facts, that property is the only source of power. They, therefore, preach that political and social reforms are but gigantic illusions and that economic reform by equalization of property must have precedence over every other kind of reform. One may join issue on every one of these premises on which rests the Socialists' case for economic reform having priority over every other kind of reform. One may contend that economic motive is not the only motive by which man is actuated. That economic power is the only kind of power no student of human society can accept. That the social status of an individual by itself often becomes a source of power and authority is made clear by the sway which the Mahatmos have held over the common man. Why do millionaires in India obey penniless Sadhus and Fakirs? Why do millions of paupers in India sell their trifling trinkets which constitute their only wealth and go to Benares and Mecca? That, religion is the source of power is illustrated by the history of India where the priest holds a sway over the common man often greater than the magistrate and where everything, even such things as strikes and elections, so easily take a religious turn and can so easily be given a religious twist. Take the case of the Plebians of Rome as a further illustration of the power of religion over man. It throws great light on this point. The Plebs had fought for a share in the supreme executive under the Roman Republic and had secured the appointment of a Plebian Consul elected by a separate electorate constituted by the *Commitia Centuriata*, which was an assembly of Piebians. They wanted a Consul of their own because they felt that the Patrician Consuls used to discriminate against the Plebians in carrying on the administration. They had apparently obtained a great gain because under the Republican Constitution of Rome one Consul had the power of vetoing an act of the other Consul. But did they in fact gain anything? The answer to this question must be in the negative. The Plebians never could get a Plebian Consul who could be said to be a strong man and who could act independently of the Patrician Consul. In the ordinary course of things the Plebians should have got a strong Plebian Consul in view of the fact that his election was to be by a separate electorate of Plebians. The question is why did they fail in getting a strong Plebian to officiate as their Consul? The answer to this question reveals the dominion which religion exercises over the minds of men. It was an accepted creed of the whole Roman *populus* that no official could enter upon the duties of his office unless the Oracle of Delphi declared that he was acceptable to the Goddess. The priests who were in charge of the temple of the Goddess of Delphi were all Patricians. Whenever therefore the Plebians elected a Consul who was known to be a strong party man opposed to the Patricians or " communal " to use the term that is current in India, the Oracle invariably declared that he was not acceptable to the Goddess. This is how the Plebians were cheated out of their rights. But what is worthy of note is that the Plebians permitted themselves to be thus cheated because they too like the Patricians, held firmly the belief that the approval of the Goddess was a condition precedent to the taking charge by an official of his duties and that election by the people was not enough. If the Plebians had contended that election was enough and that the approval by the Goddess was not necessary they would have derived the fullest benefit from the political right which they had obtained. But they did not. They agreed to elect another, less suitable to themselves but more suitable to the Goddess which in fact meant more amenable to the Patricians. Rather than give up religion, the Plebians give up material gain for which they had fought so hard. Does this not show that religion can be a source of power as great as money if not greater? The fallacy of the Socialists lies in supposing that because in the present stage of European Society property as a source of power is predominant, that the same is true of India or that the same was true of Europe in the past. Religion, social status and property are all sources of power and authority, which one man has, to control the liberty of another. One is predominant at one stage; the other is predominant at another stage. That is the only difference. If liberty is the ideal, if liberty means the destruction of the dominion which one man holds over another then obviously it cannot be insisted upon that economic reform must be the one kind of reform worthy of pursuit. If the source of power and dominion is at any given time or in any given society social and religious then social reform and religious reform must be accepted as the necessary sort of reform.

One can thus attack the doctrine of Economic Interpretation of History adopted by the Socialists of India. But I recognize that economic interpretation of history is not necessary for the validity of the Socialist contention that equalization of property is the only real reform and that it must precede everything else. However, what I like to ask the Socialists is this: Can you have economic reform without first bringing about a reform of the social order? The Socialists of India do not seem to have considered this question. I do not wish to do them an injustice. I give below a quotation from a letter which a prominent Socialist wrote a few days ago to a friend of mine in which he said, " I do not believe that we can build up a free society in India so long as there is a trace of this ill-treatment and suppression of one class by another. Believing as I do in a socialist ideal, inevitably I believe in perfect equality in the treatment of various classes and groups. I think that Socialism offers the only true remedy for this as well as other problems." Now the question that I like to ask is: Is it enough for a Socialist to say, " I believe in perfect equality in the treatment of the various classes? " To say that such a belief is enough is to disclose a complete lack of understanding of what is involved in Socialism. If Socialism is a practical programme and is not merely an ideal, distant and far off, the question for a Socialist is not whether he believes in equality. The question for him is whether he *minds* one class ill-treating and suppressing another class as a matter of system, as a matter of principle and thus allow tyranny and oppression to continue to divide one class from another. Let me analyse the factors that are involved in the realization of Socialism in order to explain fully my point. Now it is obvious that the economic reform contemplated by the Socialists cannot come about unless there is a revolution resulting in the seizure of power. That seizure of power must be by a proletariat. The first question I ask is: Will the proletariat of India combine to bring about this revolution? What will move men to such an action? It seems to me that other things being equal the only thing that will move one man to take such an action is the feeling that other man with whom he is acting are actuated by feeling of equality and fraternity and above all of justice. Men will not join in a revolution for the equalization of property unless they know that after the revolution is achieved they will be treated equally and that there will be no discrimination of caste and creed. The assurance of a socialist leading the revolution that he does not believe in caste, I am sure, will not suffice. The assurance must be the assurance proceeding from much deeper foundation, namely, the mental attitude of the compatriots towards one another in their spirit of personal equality and fraternity. Can it be said that the proletariat of India, poor as it is, recognise no distinctions except that of the rich and the poor? Can it be said that the poor in India recognize no such distinctions of caste or creed, high or low? If the fact is that they do, what unity of front can be expected from such a proletariat in its action against the rich? How can there be a revolution if the proletariat cannot present a united front? Suppose for the sake of argument that by some freak of fortune a revolution does take place and the Socialists come in power, will they not have to deal with the problems created by the particular social order prevalent in India? I can't see how a Socialist State in India can function for a second without having to grapple with the problems created by the prejudices which make Indian people observe the distinctions of high and low, clean and unclean. If Socialists are not to be content with the mouthing of fine phrases, if the Socialists wish to make Socialism a definite reality then they must recognize that the problem of social reform is fundamental and that for them there is no escape from it. That, the social order prevalent in India is a matter which a Socialist must deal with, that unless he does so he cannot achieve his revolution and that if he does achieve it as a result of good fortune he will have to grapple with it if he wishes to realize his ideal, is a proposition which in my opinion is incontrovertible. He will be compelled to take account of caste after revolution if he does not take account of it before revolution. This is only another way of saying that, turn in any direction you like, caste is the monster that crosses your path. You cannot have political reform, you cannot have economic reform, unless you kill this monster.

IV

It is a pity that Caste even today has its defenders. The defences are many. It is defended on the ground that the Caste

System is but another name for division of labour and if division of labour is a necessary feature of every civilized society then it is argued that there is nothing wrong in the Caste System. Now the first thing is to be urged against this view is that Caste System is not merely division of labour. *It is also a division of labourers.* Civilized society undoubtedly needs division of labour. But in no civilized society is division of labour accompanied by this unnatural division of labourers into watertight compartments. Caste System is not merely a division of labourers which is quite different from division of labour – it is an hierarchy in which the divisions of labourers are graded one above the other. In no other country is the division of labour accompanied by this gradation of labourers. There is also a third point of criticism against this view of the Caste System. This division of labour is not spontaneous; it is not based on natural aptitudes. Social and individual efficiency requires us to develop the capacity of an individual to the point of competency to choose and to make his own career. This principle is violated in the Caste System in so far as it involves an attempt to appoint tasks to individuals in advance, selected not on the basis of trained original capacities, but on that of the social status of the parents. Looked at from another point of view this stratification of occupations which is the result of the Caste System is positively pernicious. Industry is never static. It undergoes rapid and abrupt changes. With such changes an individual must be free to change his occupation. Without such freedom to adjust himself to changing circumstances it would be impossible for him to gain his livelihood. Now the Caste System will not allow Hindus to take to occupations where they are wanted if they do not belong to them by heredity. If a Hindu is seen to starve rather than take to new occupations not assigned to his Caste, the reason is to be found in the Caste System. By not permitting readjustment of occupations, caste becomes a direct cause of much of the unemployment we see in the country. As a form of division of labour the Caste system suffers from another serious defect. The division of labour brought about by the Caste System is not a division based on choice. Individual sentiment, individual preference has no place in it. It is based on the dogma of predestination. Considerations of social efficiency would compel us to recognize that the greatest evil in the industrial system is not: so much poverty and the suffering that it involves as the fact that so many persons have callings which make no appeal to those who are engaged in them. Such callings constantly provoke one to aversion, ill will and the desire to evade. There are many occupations in India which on account of the fact that they are regarded as degraded by the Hindus provoke those who are engaged in them to aversion. There is a constant desire to evade and escape from such occupations which arises solely because of the blighting effect which they produce upon those who follow them owing to the slight and stigma cast upon them by the Hindu religion. What efficiency can there be in a system under which neither men's hearts nor their minds are in their work? As an economic organization Caste is therefore a harmful institution, inasmuch as, it involves the subordination of man's natural powers and inclinations to the exigencies of social rules

V

Some have dug a biological trench in defence of the Caste System. It is said that the object of Caste was to preserve purity of race and purity of blood. Now ethnologists are of opinion that men of pure race exist nowhere and that there has been a mixture of all races in all parts of the world. Especially is this the case with the people of India. Mr. D. R. Bhandarkar in his paper on *Foreign Elements in the Hindu Population* has stated that " There is hardly a class, or Caste in India which has not a foreign strain in it. There is an admixture of alien blood not only among the warrior classes—the Rajputs and the Marathas—but also among the Brahmins who are under the happy delusion that they are free from all foreign elements." The Caste system cannot be said to have grown as a means of preventing the admixture of races or as a means of maintaining purity of blood. As a matter of fact Caste system came into being long after the different races of India had commingled in blood and culture. To hold that distinctions of Castes or really distinctions of race and to treat different Castes as though they were so many different races is a gross perversion of facts. What racial affinity is there between the Brahmin of the Punjab and the Brahmin of Madras? What racial affinity is there between the untouchable of Bengal and the untouchable of Madras? What racial difference is there between the Brahmin of the Punjab and the Chamar of the Punjab? What racial difference is there between the Brahmin of Madras and the Pariah of Madras? The Brahmin of the Punjab is racially of the same stock as the Chamar of the Punjab and the Brahmin of Madras is of the same race as the Pariah of Madras. Caste system does not demarcate racial division. Caste system is a social division of people of the same race. Assuming it, however, to be a case of racial divisions one may ask: What harm could there be if a mixture of races and of blood was permitted to take place in India by intermarriages between different Castes? Men are no doubt divided from animals by so deep a distinction that science recognizes men and animals as two distinct species. But even scientists who believe in purity of races do not assert that the different races constitute different species of men. They are only varieties of one and the same species. As such they can interbreed and produce an offspring which is capable of breeding and which is not sterile. An immense lot of nonsense is talked about heredity and eugenics in defence of the Caste System. Few would object to the Caste System if it was in accord with the basic principle of eugenics because few can object to the improvement of the race by judicious noting. But one fails to understand how the Caste System secures judicious mating. Caste System is a negative thing. It merely prohibits persons belonging to different Castes from intermarrying. It is not a positive method of selecting which two among a given Caste should marry. If Caste is eugenic in origin then the origin of sub-Castes must also be eugenic. But can any one seriously maintain that the origin of sub-Castes is eugenic? I think it would be absurd to contend for such a proposition and for a very obvious reason. If Caste means race then differences of sub-Castes cannot mean differences of race because sub-Castes become *ex hypothesia* sub-divisions of one and the same race. Consequently the bar against intermarrying and interdining between sub-Castes cannot be for the purpose of maintaining purity of race or of blood. If sub-Castes cannot be eugenic in origin there cannot be any substance in the contention that Caste is eugenic in origin. Again if Caste is eugenic in origin one can understand the bar against intermarriage. But what is the purpose of the interdict placed on interdining between Castes and sub-Castes alike? Interdining cannot infect blood and therefore cannot be the cause either of the improvement or of deterioration of the race. This shows that Caste has no scientific origin and that those who are attempting to give it an eugenic basis are trying to support by science what is grossly unscientific. Even today eugenics cannot become a practical possibility unless we have definite knowledge regarding the laws of heredity. Prof. Bateson in his *Mendel's Principles of Heredity* says, " There is nothing in the descent of the higher mental qualities to suggest that they follow any single system of transmission. It is likely that both they and the more marked developments of physical powers result rather from the coincidence of numerous factors than from the possession of any one genetic element." To argue that the Caste System was eugenic in its conception is to attribute to the forefathers of present-day Hindus a knowledge of heredity which even the modern scientists do not possess. A tree should be judged by the fruits it yields. If caste is eugenic what sort of a race of men it should have produced? Physically speaking the Hindus are a C3 people. They are a race of Pygmies and dwarfs stunted in stature and wanting in stamina. It is a nation 9/10ths of which is declared to be unfit for military service. This shows that the Caste System does not embody the eugenics of modern scientists. It is a social system which embodies the arrogance and selfishness of a perverse section of the Hindus who were superior enough in social status to set it in fashion and who had authority to force it on their inferiors.

VI

Caste does not result in economic efficiency. Caste cannot and has not improved the race. Caste has however done one thing. It has completely disorganized and demoralized the Hindus.

The first and foremost thing that must be recognized is that Hindu Society is a myth. The name Hindu is itself a foreign name. It was given by the Mohammedans to the natives for the purpose of distinguishing themselves. It does not occur in any Sanskrit work prior to the Mohammedan invasion. They did not feel the necessity of a common name because they had no conception of their having constituted a community. Hindu society as such does not exist. It is only a collection of castes. Each caste is conscious of its existence. Its survival is the be all and end all of its existence. Castes do not even form a federation. A caste has no feeling that it is affiliated to other castes except when there is a Hindu-Muslim riot. On all other occasions each caste endeavours to segregate itself and to distinguish itself from other castes. Each caste not only dines among itself and marries among itself but each caste prescribes its own distinctive dress. What other explanation can there be of the innumerable styles of dress worn by the men and women of India which so amuse the tourists? Indeed the ideal Hindu must be like a rat living in his own hole refusing to have any contact with others. There is an utter lack among the Hindus of what the sociologists call " consciousness of kind ". There is no Hindu consciousness of kind. In every Hindu the consciousness that exists is the consciousness of his caste. That is the reason why the Hindus cannot be said to form a society or a nation. There are however many Indians whose patriotism does not permit them to admit that Indians are not a nation, that they are only an amorphous mass of people. They have insisted that underlying the apparent diversity there is a fundamental unity which marks the life of the Hindus in as much as there is a similarity of habits and customs, beliefs and thoughts which obtain all over the continent of India. Similarity in habits and customs, beliefs and thoughts there is. But one cannot accept the conclusion that therefore, the Hindus constitute a society. To do so is to misunderstand the essentials which go to make up a society. Men do not become a society by living in physical proximity any more than a man ceases to be a member of his society by living so many miles away from other men. Secondly similarity in habits and customs, beliefs and thoughts is not enough to constitute men into society. Things may be passed physically from one to another like bricks. In the same way habits and customs, beliefs and thoughts of one group may be taken over by another group and there may thus appear a similarity between the two. Culture spreads by diffusion and that is why one finds similarity between various primitive tribes in the matter of their habits and customs, beliefs and thoughts, although they do not live in proximity. But no one could say that because there was this similarity the primitive tribes constituted one society. This is because similarly in certain things is not enough to constitute a society. Men constitute a society because they have things which they possess in common. To have similar thing is totally different from possessing things in common. And the only way by which men can come to possess things in common with one another is by being in communication with one another. This is merely another way of saying that Society continues to exist by communication indeed in communication. To make it concrete, it is not enough if men act in a way which agrees with the acts of others. Parallel activity, even if similar, is not sufficient to bind men into a society. This is proved by the fact that the festivals observed by the different Castes amongst the Hindus are the same. Yet these parallel performances of similar festivals by the different castes have not bound them into one integral whole. For that purpose what is necessary is for a man to share and participate in a common activity so that the same emotions are aroused in him that animate the others. Making the individual a sharer or partner in the associated activity so that he feels its success as his success, its failure as his failure is the real thing that binds men and makes a society of them. The Caste System prevents common activity and by preventing common activity it has prevented the Hindus from becoming a society with a unified life and a consciousness of its own being.

VII

The Hindus often complain of the isolation and exclusiveness of a gang or a clique and blame them for anti-social spirit. But they conveniently forget that this anti-social spirit is the worst feature of their own Caste System. One caste enjoys singing a hymn of hate against another caste as much as the Germans did in singing their hymn of hate against the English during the last war. The literature of the Hindus is full of caste genealogies in which an attempt is made to give a noble origin to one caste and an ignoble origin to other castes. The *Sahyadrikhand* is a notorious instance of this class of literature. This anti-social spirit is not confined to caste alone. It has gone deeper and has poisoned the mutual relations of the sub-castes as well. In my province the Golak Brahmins, Deorukha Brahmins, Karada Brahmins, Palshe Brahmins and Chitpavan Brahmins, all claim to be sub-divisions of the Brahmin Caste. But the anti-social spirit that prevails between them is quite as marked and quite as virulent as the anti-social spirit that prevails between them and other non-Brahmin castes. There is nothing strange in this. An anti-social spirit is found wherever one group has " interests of its own " which shut it out from full interaction with other groups, so that its prevailing purpose is protection of what it has got. This anti-social spirit, this spirit of protecting its own interests is as much a marked feature of the different castes in their isolation from one another as it is of nations in their isolation. The Brahmin's primary concern is to protect " his interest " against those of the non-Brahmins and the non-Brahmin's primary concern is to protect their interests against those of the Brahmins. The Hindus, therefore, are not merely an assortment of castes but they are so many warring groups each living for itself and for its selfish ideal. There is another feature of caste which is deplorable. The ancestors of the present-day English fought on one side or the other in the wars of the Roses and the Cromwellian War. But the decendents of those who fought on the one side do not bear any animosity— any grudge against the descendents of those who fought on the other side. The feud is forgotten. But the present-day non-Brahmins cannot forgive the present-day Brahmins for the insult their ancestors gave to Shivaji. The present-day Kayasthas will not forgive the present-day Brahmins for the infamy cast upon their forefathers by the forefathers of the latter. To what is this difference due? Obviously to the Caste System. The existence of Caste and Caste Consciousness has served to keep the memory of past feuds between castes green and has prevented solidarity.

VIII

The recent discussion about the excluded and partially included areas has served to draw attention to the position of what are called the aboriginal tribes in India. They number about 13 millions if not more. Apart from the questions whether their exclusion from the new Constitution is proper or improper, the fact still remains that these aborigines have remained in their primitive uncivilized State in a land which boasts of a civilization thousands of years old. Not only are they not civilized but some of them follow pursuits which have led to their being classified as criminals. Thirteen millions of people living in the midst of civilization are still in a savage state and are leading the life of hereditary criminals! ! But the Hindus have never felt ashamed of it. This is a phenomenon which in my view is quite unparalleled. What is the cause of this shameful state of affairs? Why has no attempt been made to civilize these aborigines and to lead them to take to a more honourable way of making a living? The Hindus will probably seek to account for this savage state of the aborigines by attributing to them congenital stupidity. They will probably not admit that the aborigines have remained savages because they had made no effort to civilize them, to give them medical aid, to reform them, to make them good citizens. But supposing a Hindu wished to do what the Christian missionary is doing for these aborigines, could he have done it? I submit not. Civilizing the aborigines means adopting them as your own, living in their midst, and cultivating fellow-feeling, in short loving them. How is it possible for a Hindu to do this? His whole life is one anxious effort to preserve his caste. Caste is his precious possession which he must save at any cost. He cannot consent to lose it by establishing contact with the aborigines the remnants of the hateful Anary as of the *Vedic* days. Not that a Hindu could not *be* taught the sense of duty to fallen humanity, but the trouble is that no amount of sense of duty can enable him to overcome his duty to preserve his caste. Caste is, therefore, the real explanation as to why the Hindu has let the savage remain a savage in the midst of his civilization without blushing or without feeling any sense of remorse or repentance. The Hindu has not realized that these aborigines are a source of potential danger. If these savages remain savages they may not do any harm to the Hindus. But if they are reclaimed by non-Hindus and converted to their faiths they will swell the ranks of the enemies of the Hindus. If this happens the Hindu will have to thank himself and his Caste System.

IX

Not only has the Hindu made no effort for the humanitarian cause of civilizing the savages but the higher-caste Hindus have deliberately prevented the lower castes who are within the pale of Hinduism from rising to the cultural leve. of the higher castes. 1. will give two instances, one of the Sonars and the other of the Pathare Prabhus. Both are communities quite well-known in Maharashtra. Like the rest of the communities desiring to raise their status these two communities were at one time endeavouring to adopt some of the ways and habits of the Brahmins. The Sonars were styling themselves Daivadnya Brahmins and were wearing their " dhotis " with folds on and using the word *namaskar* for salutation. Both, the folded way of wearing the " dhoti " and the *namaskar* were special to the Brahmins. The Brahmins did not like this imitation and this attempt by Sonars to pass off as Brahmins. Under the authority of the Peshwas the Brahmins successfully put down this attempt on the part. of the Sonars to adopt the ways of the Brahmins. They even got the President of the Councils of the East India Company's settlement in Bombay to issue a. prohibitory order against the Sonars residing in Bombay. At one time the Pathare Prabhus had widow-remarriage as a custom of their caste. This custom of widow-remarriage was later on looked upon as amark of social inferiority by some members of the caste especially because it was contrary to the custom prevalent among the Brahmins. With the object of raising the status of their community some Pathare Prabhus sought to stop this practice of widow-remarriage that was prevalent in their caste. The community was divided into two camps, one for and the other against the innovation. The Peshwas took the side of those in favour of widow-remarriage and thus virtually prohibited the Pathare Prabhus from following the ways of the Brahmins. The Hindus criticise the Mohammedans for having spread their religion by the use of the sword. They also ridicule Christianity on the score of the inquisition. But really speaking who is better and more worthy of our respect—the Mohammedans and Christians who attempted to thrust down the throats of unwilling persons what they regarded as necessary for their salvation or the Hindu who would not spread the light, who would endeavour to keep others in darkness, who would not consent to share his intellectual and social inheritance with those who are ready and willing to make it a part of their own make-up? I have no hesitation in saying that if the Mohammedan has been cruel the Hindu has been mean and meanness is worse than cruelty.

X

Whether the Hindu religion was or was not a missionary religion has been a controversial issue. Some hold the view that it was never a missionary religion. Others hold that it was. That the Hindu religion was once a missionary religion must be admitted. It could not have spread over the face of India, if it was not a missionary religion. That today it is not a missionary religion is also a fact which must be accepted. The question therefore is not whether or not the Hindu religion was a missionary religion. The real question is why did the Hindu religion cease to be a missionary religion? My answer is this. Hindu religion ceased to be a missionary religion when the Caste System grew up among the Hindus. Caste is inconsistent with conversion. Inculcation of beliefs and dogmas is not the only problem that is involved in conversion. To find a place for the convert in the social life of the community is another and a much more important problem that arises in connection with conversion. That problem is where to place the convert, in what caste? It is a problem which must baffle every Hindu wishing to make aliens converts to his religion. Unlike the club the membership of a caste is not open to all and sundry. The law of caste confines its membership to person born in the caste. Castes are autonomous and there is no authority anywhere to compel a caste to admit a new-comer to its social life. Hindu Society being a collection of castes and each caste being a close corporation there is no place for a convert. Thus it is the caste which has prevented the Hindus from expanding and from absorbing other religious communities. So long as caste remain, Hindu religion cannot be made a missionary religion and *Shudhi* will be both a folly and a futility.

XI

The reasons which have made *Shudhi* impossible for Hindus are also responsible for making *Sanghatan* impossible. The idea underlying *Sanghalan* is to remove from the mind of the Hindu that timidity and cowardice which so painfully make him off from the Mohammedan and the Sikh and which have led him to adopt the low ways of treachery and cunning for protecting himself. The question naturally arises: From where does the Sikh or the Mohammedan derive his strength which makes him brave and fearless? I am sure it is not due to relative superiority of physical strength, diet or drill. It is due to the strength arising out of the feeling that all Sikhs will come to the rescue of a Sikh when he is in danger and that all Mohammedans will rush to save a Muslim if he is attacked. The Hindu can derive no such strength. He cannot feel assured that his fellows will come to his help. Being one and fated to be alone he remains powerless, develops timidity and cowardice and in a fight surrenders or runs away. The Sikh as well as the Muslim stands fearless and gives battle because he knows that though one he will not be alone. The presence of this belief in the one helps him to hold out and the absence of it in the other makes him to give way. If you pursue this matter further and ask what is it that enables the Sikh and the Mohammedan to feel so assured and why is the Hindu filled with such despair in the matter of help and assistance you will find that the reasons for this difference lie in the difference in their associated mode of living. The associated mode of life practised by the Sikhs and the Mohammedans produces fellow-feeling. The associated mode of life of the Hindus does not. Among Sikhs and Muslims there is a social cement which makes them *Bhais*. Among Hindus there is no such cement and one Hindu does not regard another Hindu as his *Bhai*. This explains why a Sikh says and feels that one

Sikh, or one Khalsa is equal to *Sava Lakh* men. This explains why one Mohammedan is equal to a crowd of Hindus. This difference is undoubtedly a difference due to caste. So long as caste remains, there will be no *Sanghalan* and so long as there is no *Sanghatan* the Hindu will remain weak and meek. The Hindus claim to be a very tolerant people. In my opinion this is a mistake. On many occasions they can be intolerant and if on some occasions they are tolerant that is because they are too weak to oppose or too indifferent to oppose. This indifference of the Hindus has become so much a part of their nature that a Hindu will quite meekly tolerate an insult as well as a wrong. You see amongst them, to use the words of Morris, " *The great reading down the little, the strong beating down the weak, cruel men fearing not, kind men daring not and wise men caring not.*" With the Hindu Gods all forbearing, it is not difficult to imagine the pitiable condition of the wronged and the oppressed among the Hindus. Indifferentism is the worst kind of disease that can infect a people. Why is the Hindu so indifferent? In my opinion this indifferentism is the result of Caste System which has made *Sanghatan* and co-operation even for a good cause impossible.

XII

The assertion by the individual of his own opinions and beliefs, his own independence and interest as over against group standards, group authority and group interests is the beginning of all reform. But whether the reform will continue depends upon what scope the group affords for such individual assertion. If the group is tolerant and fair-minded in dealing with such individuals they will continue to assert and in the end succeed in converting their fellows. On the other hand if the group is intolerant and does not bother about the means it adopts to stifle such individuals they will perish and the reform will die out. Now a caste has an unquestioned right to excommunicate any man who is guilty of breaking the rules of the caste and when it is realized that excommunication involves a complete cesser of social intercourse it will be agreed that as a form of punishment there is really little to choose between excommunication and death. No wonder individual Hindus have not had the courage to assert their independence by breaking the barriers of caste. It is true that man cannot get on with his fellows. But it is also true that he cannot do without them. He would like to have the society of his fellows on his terms. If be cannot get it on his terms then he will be ready to have it on any terms even amounting to complete surrender. This is because he cannot do without society. A caste is ever ready to take advantage of the helplessness of a man and insist upon complete conformity to its code in letter and in spirit. A caste can easily organize itself into a conspiracy to make the life of a reformer a hell and if a conspiracy is a crime I do not understand why such a nefarious act as an attempt to excommunicate a person for daring to act contrary to the rules of caste should not be made an offence punishable in law. But as it is, even law gives each caste an autonomy to regulate its membership and punish dissenters with excommunication. Caste in the hands of the orthodox has been a powerful weapon for persecuting the reforms and for killing all reform.

XIII

The effect of caste on the ethics of the Hindus is simply deplorable. Caste has killed public spirit. Caste has destroyed the sense of public charity. Caste has made public opinion impossible. A Hindu's public is his caste. His responsibility is only to his caste. His loyalty is restricted only to his caste. Virtue has become caste-ridden and morality has become, caste-bound. There is no sympathy to the deserving. There is no appreciation of the meritorious. There is no charity to the needy. Suffering as such calls for no response. There is charity but it begins with the caste and ends with the caste. There *is* sympathy but not for men of other caste. Would a Hindu acknowledge and follow the leadership of a great and good man? The case of a Mahatma apart, the answer must be that he will follow a leader if he is a man of his caste. A Brahmin will follow a leader only if he is a Brahmin, a Kayastha if he is a Kayastha and so on. The capacity to appreciate merits in a man apart from his caste does not exist in a Hindu. There is appreciation of virtue but only when the man is a fellow caste-man. The whole morality is as bad as tribal morality. My caste-man, right or wrong; my caste-man, good or bad. It is not a case of standing by virtue and not standing by vice. It is a case of standing or not standing by the caste. Have not Hindus committed treason against their country in the interests of their caste?

XIV

I would not be surprised if some of you have grown weary listening to this tiresome tale of the sad effects which caste has produced. There is nothing new in it. I will therefore turn to the constructive side of the problem. What is your ideal society if you do not want caste is a question that is bound to be asked of you. If you ask me, my ideal would be a society based on *Liberty, Equality* and *Fraternity*. And why not? What objection can there be to Fraternity? I cannot imagine any. An ideal society should be mobile, should be full of channels for conveying a change taking place in one part to other parts. In an ideal society there should be many interests consciously communicated and shared. There should be varied and free points of contact with other modes of association. In other words there must be social endosmosis. This is fraternity, which is only another name for democracy. Democracy is not merely a form of Government. It is primarily a mode of associated living, of conjoint communicated experience. It is essentially an attitude of respect and reverence towards fellowmen. Any objection to Liberty? Few object to liberty in the sense of a right to free movement, in the sense of a right to life and limb. There is no objection to liberty in the sense of a right to property, tools and materials as being necessary for earning a living to keep the body in due state of health. Why not allow liberty to benefit by an effective and competent use of a person's powers? The supporters of caste who would allow liberty in the sense of a right to life, limb and property, would not readily consent to liberty in this sense, inasmuch as it involves liberty to choose one's profession. But to object to this kind of liberty is to perpetuate slavery. For slavery does not merely mean a legalized form of subjection. It means a state of society in which some men are forced to accept from other the purposes which control their conduct. This condition obtains even where there is no slavery in the legal sense. It is found where, as in the Caste System, some persons are compelled to carry on certain prescribed callings which are not of their choice. Any objection to equality? This has obviously been the most contentious part of the slogan of the French Revolution. The objections to equality may be sound and one may have to admit that all men are not equal. But what of that? Equality may be a fiction but nonetheless one must accept it as the governing principle. A. man's power is dependent upon (1) physical heredity, (2) social inheritance or endowment in the form of parental care, education, accumulation of scientific knowledge, everything which enables him to be more efficient than the savage, and finally, (3) on his own efforts. In all these three respects men are undoubtedly unequal. But the question is, shall we treat them as unequal because they are unequal? This is a question which the opponents of equality must answer. From the standpoint of the individualist it may be just to treat men unequally so far as their efforts are unequal. It may be desirable to give as much incentive as possible to the full development of every one's powers. But what would happen if men were treated unequally as they are, in the first two respects? It is obvious that those individuals also in whose favour there is birth, education, family name, business connections and inherited wealth would be selected in the race. But selection under such circumstances would not be a selection of the able. It would be the selection of the privileged. The reason therefore, which forces that in the third respect we should treat men unequally demands that in the first two respects we should treat men as equally as possible. On the other hand it can be urged that if it is good for the social body to get the most out of its members, it can get most out of them only by making them equal as far as possible at the very start of the race. That is one reason why we cannot escape equality. But there is another reason why we must accept equality. A Statesman is concerned with vast numbers of people. He has neither the time nor the knowledge to draw fine distinctions and to treat each equitably *i.e.* according to need or according to capacity. However desirable or reasonable an equitable treatment of men may be, humanity is not capable of assortment and classification. The statesman, therefore, must follow some rough and ready rule and that rough and ready rule is to treat all men alike not because they are alike but because classification and assortment is impossible. The doctrine of equality is glaringly fallacious but taking all in all it is the only way a statesman can proceed in politics which is a severely practical affair and which demands a severely practical test.

XV

But there is a set of reformers who hold out a different ideal. They go by the name of the Arya Samajists and their ideal of social organization is what is called Chaturvarnya or the division of society into four classes instead of the four thousand castes that we have in India. To make it more attractive and to disarm opposition the protagonists of Chaturvarnya take great care to point out that their Chaturvarnya is based not on birth but on *guna* (worth). At the outset, I must confess that notwithstanding the worth-basis of this Chaturvarnya, it is an ideal to which I cannot reconcile myself. In the first place, if under the Chaturvarnya of the Arya Samajists an individual is to take his place in the Hindu Society according to his worth. I do not understand why the Arya Samajists insist upon labelling men as Brahmin, Kshatriya, Vaishya and Shudra. A learned man would be honoured without his being labelled a Brahmin. A soldier would be respected without his being designated a Kshatriya. If European society honours its soldiers and its servants without giving them permanent labels, why should Hindu Society find it difficult to do so is a question, which Arya Samajists have not cared to consider. There is another objection to the continuance of these labels. All reform consists in a change in the notions, sentiment and mental attitudes of the people towards men and things. It is common experience that certain names become associated with certain notions and sentiments, which determine a person's attitude towards men and things. The names, Brahmin, Kshatriya, Vaishya and Shudra, are names which are associated with a definite and fixed notion in the mind of every Hindu. That notion is that of a hierarchy based on birth. So long as these names continue, Hindus will continue to think of the Brahmin, Kshatriya, Vaishya and Shudra as hierarchical divisions of high and low, based on birth, and act accordingly. The Hindu must be made to unlearn all this. But how can this happen if the old labels remain and continue to recall to his mind old notions. If new notions are to be inculcated in the minds of people it is necessary to give them new names.

To continue the old name is to make the reform futile. To allow this Chaturvarnya, based on worth to be designated by such stinking labels of Brahmin, Kshatriya, Vaishya, Shudra, indicative of social divisions based on birth, is a snare.

XVI

To me this Chaturvarnya with its old labels is utterly repellent and my whole being rebels against it. But I do not wish to rest my objection to Chaturvarnya on mere grounds of sentiments. There are more solid grounds on which I rely for my opposition to it. A close examination of this ideal has convinced me that as a system of social organization, Chaturvarnya is impracticable, harmful and has turned out to be a miserable failure. From a practical point of view, the system of Chaturvarnya raises several difficulties which its protagonists do not seem to have taken into account. The principle underlying caste is fundamentally different from the principle underlying *Varna*. Not only are they fundamentally different but they are also fundamentally opposed. The former is based on worth . How are you going to compel people who have acquired a higher status based on birth without reference to their worth to vacate that status? How are you going to compel people to recognize the status due to a man in accordance with his worth, who is occupying a lower status based on his birth? For this you must first break up the caste System, in order to be able to establish the *Varna* system. How are you going to reduce the four thousand castes, based oil birth, to the four *Varnas*, based on worth? This is the first difficulty which the protagonists of the Chaturvarnya must grapple with. There is a second difficulty which the protagonists of Chaturvarnya must grapple with, if they wish to make the establishment of Chaturvarnya a success.

Chaturvarnya pre-supposes that you can classify people into four definite classes. Is this possible? In this respect, the ideal of Chaturvarnya has, as you will see, a close affinity to the Platonic ideal. To Plato, men fell by nature into three classes. In some individuals, he believed mere appetites dominated. He assigned them to the labouring and trading classes. Others revealed to him that over and above appetites, they have a courageous disposition. He classed them as defenders in war and guardians of internal peace. Others showed a capacity to grasp the universal reason underlying things. He made them the law-givers of the people. The criticism to which Plato's Republic is subject, is also the criticism which must apply to the system of Chaturvarnya, in so far as it proceeds upon the possibility of an accurate classification of men into four distinct classes. The chief criticism against Plato is that his idea of lumping of individuals into a few sharply marked-off classes is a very superficial view of man and his powers. Plato had no perception of the uniqueness of every individual, of his incommensurability with others, of each individual forming a class of his own. He had no recognition of the infinite diversity of active tendencies and combination of tendencies of which an individual is capable. To him, there were types of faculties or powers in the individual constitution. All this is demonstrably wrong. Modem science has shown that lumping together of individuals into a few sharply marked-off classes is a superficial view of man not worthy of serious consideration. Consequently, the utilization of the qualities of individuals is incompatible with their stratification by classes, since the qualities of individuals are so variable. Chaturvarnya must fail for the very reason for which Plato's Republic must fail, namely that it is not possible to pigeon men into holes, according as he belongs to one class or the other. That it is impossible to accurately classify people into four definite classes is proved by the fact that the original four classes have now become four thousand castes.

There is a third difficulty in the way of the establishment of the system of Chaturvarnya. How are you going to maintain the system of Chaturvarnya, supposing it was established? One important requirement for the successful working of Chaturvarnya is the maintenance of the penal system which could maintain it by its sanction. The system of Chaturvarnya must perpetually face the problem of the transgressor. Unless there is a penalty attached to the act of transgression, men will not keep to their respective classes. The whole system will break down, being contrary to human nature. Chaturvarnya cannot subsist by its own inherent goodness. It must be enforced by law.

That, without penal sanction the ideal of Chaturvarnya cannot be realized, is proved by the story in the Ramayana of Rama killing Shambuka. Some people seem to blame Rama because he wantonly and without reason killed Shambuka. But to blame Rama for killing Shambuka is to misunderstand the whole situation. Ram Raj was a Raj based on Chaturvarnya. As a king, Rama was bound to maintain Chaturvarnya. It was his duty therefore to kill Shambuka, the Shudra, who had transgressed his class and wanted to be a Brahmin. This is the reason why Rama killed Shambuka. But this also shows that penal sanction is necessary for the maintenance of Chaturvarnya. Not only penal sanction is necessary, but penalty of death is necessary. That is why Rama did not inflict on Shambuka a lesser punishment. That is why Manu-Smriti prescribes such heavy sentences as cutting off the tongue or pouring of molten lead in the ears of the Shudra, who recites or hears the *Veda*. The supporters of Chaturvarnya must give an assurance that they could successfully classify men and they could induce modern society in the twentieth century to reforge the penal sanctions of Manu-Smriti.

The protagonists of Chaturvarnya do not seem to have considered what is to happen to women in their system. Are they also to be divided into four classes, Brahmin, Kshatriya, Vaishya and Shudra? Or are they to be allowed to take the status of their husbands. If the status of the woman is to be the consequence of marriage what becomes of the underlying principle of Chaturvarnya, namely, that the status of a person should be based upon the worth of that person? If they are to be classified according to their worth is their classification to be nominal or real? If it is to be nominal then it is useless and then the protagonists of Chaturvarnya must admit that their system does not apply to women. If it is real, are the protagonists of Chaturvarnya prepared to follow the logical consequences of applying it to women? They must be prepared to have women priests and women soldiers. Hindu society has grown accustomed to women teachers and women barristers. It may grow accustomed to women brewers and women butchers. But he would be a bold person, who would say that it will allow women priests and women soldiers. But that will be the logical outcome of applying Chaturvarnya to women. Given these difficulties, I think no one except a congenital idiot could hope and believe in a successful regeneration of the Chaturvarnya.

XVII

Assuming that Chaturvarnya is practicable, I contend that it is the most vicious system. That the Brahmins should cultivate knowledge, that the Kshatriya should bear arms, that the Vaishya. should trade and that the Shudra should serve sounds as though it was a system of division of labour. Whether the theory was intended to state that the Shudra *need not* or that whether it was intended to lay down that he *must not*, is an interesting question. The defenders of Chaturvarnya give it the first meaning. They say, why should the Shudra need trouble to acquire wealth, when the three *Varnas* are there to support him? Why need the Shudra bother to take to education, when there is the Brahmin to whom he can go when the occasion for reading or writing arises? Why need the Shudra worry to arm himself because there is the Kshatriya to protect him? The theory of Chaturvarnya, understood in this sense, may be said to look upon the Shudra as the ward and the three *Varnas as* his guardians. Thus interpreted, it is a simple, elevating and alluring theory. Assuming this to be the correct view of the underlying conception of Chaturvarnya, it seems to me that the system is neither fool-proof nor knave-proof. What is to happen, if the Brahmins, Vaishyas and Kshatriyas fail to pursue knowledge, to engage in economic enterprise and to be efficient soldiers which are their respective functions? Contrary-wise, suppose that they discharge their functions but flout their duty to the Shudra or to one another, what is to happen to the Shudra if the three classes refuse to support him on fair terms or combine to keep him down? Who is to safeguard the interests of the Shudra or for the matter of that of the Vaishya and Kshatriya when the person, who is trying to take advantage of his ignorance is the Brahmin? Who is to defend the liberty of the Shudra and for the matter of that, of the Brahmin and the Vaishya when the person who is robbing him of it is the Kshatriya? Inter-dependence of one class on another class is inevitable. Even dependence of one class upon another may sometimes become allowable. But why make one person depend upon another in the matter of his vital needs? Education everyone must have. Means of defence everyone must have. These are the paramount requirements of every man for his self-preservation. How can the fact that his neighbour is educated and armed help a man who is uneducated and disarmed. The whole theory is absurd. These are the questions, which the defenders of Chaturvarnya do not seem to be troubled about. But they are very pertinent questions. Assuming their conception of Chaturvarnya that the relationship between the different classes is that of ward and guardian is the real conception underlying Chaturvarnya, it must be admitted that it makes no provision to safeguard the interests of the ward from the misdeeds of the guardian. Whether the relationship of guardian and ward was the real underlying conception, on which Chaturvarnya was based, there is no doubt that in practice the relation was that of master and servants. The three classes, Brahmins, Kshatriyas and Vaishyas although not very happy in their mutual relationship managed to work by compromise. The Brahmin flattered the Kshatriya and both let the Vaishya live in order to be able to live upon him. But the three agreed to beat down the Shudra. He was not allowed to acquire wealth lest he should be independent of the three *Varncus*. He was prohibited from acquiring knowledge lest he should keep a steady vigil regarding his interests. He was prohibited from bearing arms lest he should have the means to rebel against their authority. That this is how the Shudras were treated by the Tryavarnikas is evidenced by the Laws of Manu. There is no code of laws more infamous regarding social rights than the Laws of Manu. Any instance from anywhere of social injustice must pale before it. Why have the mass of people tolerated the social evils to which they have been subjected? There have been social revolutions in other countries of the world. Why have there not been social revolutions in India is a question which has incessantly troubled me. There is only one answer, which I can give and it is that the lower classes of Hindus have been completely disabled for direct action on account of this wretched system of Chaturvarnya. They could not bear arms and without arms they could not rebel. They were all ploughmen or rather condemned to be ploughmen and they never were allowed to convert their ploughshare into swords. They had no bayonets and therefore everyone who chose could and did sit upon them. On account of the Chaturvarnya, they could receive no education. They could not think out or know the way to their salvation. They were condemned to be lowly and not knowing the way of escape and not having the means of escape, they became reconciled to eternal servitude, which they accepted as their inescapable fate. It is true that even in Europe the strong has not shrunk from the exploitation, nay the spoliation of the weak. But in Europe, the strong have never contrived to make the weak helpless against exploitation so shamelessly as was the case in India among the Hindus. Social war has been raging between the strong and the weak far more violently in Europe than it has ever been in India. Yet, the weak in Europe has had in his freedom of military service his *physical weapon,* in suffering his *political weapon* and in education his *moral weapon.* These three weapons for emancipation were never withheld by the strong from the weak in Europe. All these weapons were, however, denied to the masses in India by Chaturvarnya. There cannot be a more degrading system of social organization than the Chaturvarnya. It is the system which deadens, paralyses and cripples the people from helpful activity. This is no exaggeration. History bears ample evidence. There is only one period in Indian history which is a period of freedom, greatness and glory. That is the period of the Mourya Empire. At all other times the country suffered from defeat and darkness. But the Mourya period was a period when Chaturvarnya was completely annihilated, when the Shudras, who constituted the mass of the people, came into their own and became the rulers of the country. The period of defeat and darkness is the period when Chaturvarnya flourished to the damnation of the greater part of the people of the country.

XVIII

Chaturvarnya is not new. It is as old as the *Vedas*. That is one of the reasons why we are asked by the Arya Samajists to consider its claims. Judging from the past as a system of social organization, it has been tried and it has failed. How many times have the Brahmins annihilated the seed of the Kshatriyas! How many times have the Kshatriyas annihilated the Brahmins! The Mahabharata and the Puranas are full of incidents of the strife between the Brahmins and the Kshatriyas. They even quarrèled over such petty questions as to who should salute first, as to who should give way first, the Brahmins or the Kshatriyas, when the two met in the street. Not only was the Brahmin an eyesore to die Kshatriya and the Kshatriya an eyesore to the Brahmin, it seems that the Kshatriyas had become tyrannical and the masses, disarmed as they were under the system of Chaturvarnya, were praying Almighty God for relief from their tyranny. The Bhagwat tells us very definitely that Krishna had taken Avtar for one sacred purpose and that was to annihilate the Kshatriyas. With these instances of rivalry and enmity between the different *Vurnas* before us, I do not understand how any one can hold out Chaturvarnya as an ideal to be aimed at or as a pattern, on which the Hindu Society should be remodelled.

XIX

I have dealt with those, who are without you and whose hostility to your ideal is quite open. There appear to be others, who are neither without you nor with you. I was hesitating whether I should deal with their point of view. But on further consideration I have come to the conclusion that I must and that for two reasons. Firstly, their attitude to the problem of caste is not merely an attitude of neutrality, but is an attitude of aimed neutrality. Secondly, they probably represent a considerable body of people. Of these, there is one set which finds nothing peculiar nor odious in the Caste System of the Hindus. Such Hindus cite the case of Muslims, Sikhs and Christians and find comfort in the fact that they too have castes amongst them. In considering this question you must at the outset bear in mind that nowhere is human society *one* single whole. It is always plural. In the world of action, the individual is one limit and society the other. Between them lie all sorts of associative arrangements of lesser and larger scope, families, friendship, co-operative associations, business combines, political parties, bands of thieves and robbers. These small groups are usually firmly welded together and are often as exclusive as castes. They have a narrow and intensive code, which is often anti-social. This is true of every society, in Europe as well as in Asia, The question to be asked in determining whether a given society is an ideal society; is not whether there are groups in it, because groups exist in all societies. The. questions to be asked in determining what is an ideal society are: How numerous and varied are the interests which are consciously shared by the groups? How full and free is the interplay with other forms of associations? Are the forces that separate groups and classes more numerous than the forces that unite? What social significance is attached to this group life? Is its exclusiveness a matter of custom and convenience or is it a matter of religion? It is in the light of these questions that one must decide whether caste among Non-Hindus is the same as caste among Hindus. If we apply these considerations to castes among Mohammedans, Sikhs and Christians on the one hand and to castes among Hindus on the other, you will find that caste among Non-Hindus is fundamentally different from caste among Hindus. First, the ties, which consciously make the Hindus hold together, are non-existent, while among Non-Hindus there are many that hold them together. The strength of a society depends upon the presence of points of contact, possibilities of interaction between different groups which exist in it. These are what Carlyle calls " organic filaments " *i.e.* the elastic threads which help to bring the disintegrating elements together and to reunite them. There is no integrating farce among the Hindus to counteract the disintegration caused by caste. While among the Non-Hindus there are plenty of these organic filaments which bind' them together. Again it must be borne in mind that although there are castes among Non-Hindus, as there are among Hindus, caste has not the same social significance for Non-Hindus as it has for Hindus. Ask Mohammedan or a Sikh, who he is? He tells you that he is a Mohammedan or a Sikh as the case may be. He does not tell you his caste although he has one and you are satisfied with his answer. When he tells you that he is a Muslim, you do not proceed to ask him whether he is a Shiya or a Suni; Sheikh or Saiyad; Khatik or Pinjari. When he tells you he is a Sikh, you do not ask him whether he is Jat or Roda; Mazbi or Ramdasi. But you are not satisfied, if a person tells you that he is a Hindu. You feel bound to inquire into his caste. Why? Because so essential is caste in the case of a Hindu that without knowing it you do not feel sure what sort of a being he is. That caste has not the same social significance among Non-Hindus as it has among Hindus is clear if you take into consideration the consequences which follow breach of caste. There may be castes among Sikhs and Mohammedans but the Sikhs and the Mohammedans will not outcast a Sikh or a Mohammedan if he broke his caste. Indeed, the very idea of excommunication is foreign to the Sikhs and the Mohammedans. But with the Hindus the case is entirely different. He is sure to be outcasted if he broke caste. This shows the difference in the social significance of caste to Hindus and Non-Hindus. This is the second point of difference. But there is also a third and a more important one.

Caste among the non-Hindus has no religious consecration; but among the Hindus most decidedly it has. Among the Non-Hindus, caste is only a practice, not a sacred institution. They did not originate it. With them it is only a survival. They do not regard caste as a religious dogma. Religion compels the Hindus to treat isolation and segregation of castes as a virtue. Religion does not compel the Non-Hindus to take the same attitude towards caste. If Hindus wish to break caste, their religion will come in their way. But it will not be so in the case of Non-Hindus. It is, therefore, a dangerous delusion to take comfort in the mere existence of caste among Non-Hindus, without caring to know what place caste occupies in their life and whether there are other " organic filaments ", which subordinate the feeling of caste to the feeling of community. The sooner the Hindus are cured of this delusion the butter.

The other set denies that caste presents any problem at all for the .Hindus to consider. Such Hindus seek comfort in the view that the Hindus have survived and take this as a proof of their fitness to survive. This point of view is well expressed by Prof. S. Radhakrishnan in his *Hindu view of life*. Referring to Hinduism he says, " The civilization itself has not, been a short-lived one. its historic records date back for over four thousand years and even then it had reached a stage of civilization which has continued its unbroken, though at times slow and static, course until the present day. It has stood the stress and strain of more than four or five millenniums of spiritual thought and experience. Though peoples of different races and cultures have *been* pouring into India from the dawn of History, Hinduism has been able to maintain its supremacy and even the proselytising creeds backed by political power have not been able to coerce the large majority of Hindus to their views. The Hindu culture possesses some vitality which seems to be denied to some other more forceful current . It is no more necessary to dissect Hinduism than to open a tree to see whether the sap still runs." The name of Prof. Radhakrishnan is big enough to invest with profundity whatever he says and impress the minds of his readers. But I must not hesitate to speak out my mind. For, I fear that his statement may become the basis of a vicious argument that the fact of survival is proof of fitness to survive. It seems to me that the question is. not whether a community lives or dies; the question is on what plane does it live. There are different modes of survival. But all are not equally honourable. For an individual as well as for a society, there is a gulf between merely living and living worthily. To fight in a battle and to live in glory is one mode. To beat a retreat, to surrender and to live the life of a captive is. also a mode of survival. It is useless for a Hindu to take comfort in the fact that he and his people have survived. What he must consider is what is the quality of their survival. If he does that, I am sure he will cease to take pride in the mere fact of survival. A Hindu's life has been a life of continuous defeat and what appears to him to be life everlasting is not living everlastingly but is really a life which is perishing everlastingly. It is a mode of survival of which every right-minded Hindu, who is not afraid to own up the truth, will feel ashamed.

XX

There is no doubt; in my opinion, that unless you change your social order you can achieve little by way of progress. You cannot mobilize the community either for defence or for offence. You cannot build anything on the foundations of caste. You cannot build up a nation, you cannot build up a morality. Anything that you will build on the foundations of caste will crack and will never be a whole.

The only question that remains to be considered is — *How to bring about the reform of the Hindu social order? How to abolish caste?* This is a question of supreme importance. There is a view that in the refarm of caste, the first step to take, is to abolish sub-castes. This view is based upon the supposition that there is a greater similarity in manners and status between sub-caste than there is between castes. I think, this is an erroneous supposition. The Brahmins of Northern and Central India are socially of lower grade, as compared with the Brahmins of the Deccan and Southern India. The former are only cooks and water-carriers while the latter occupy a high social position. On the other hand, in Northern India, the Vaishyas and Kayasthas are intellectually and socially on a par with the Brahmins of the Deccan and Southern India. Again, in the matter of food there is no similarity between the Brahmins of the Deccan and Southern India, who are vegetarians and the Brahmins of Kashmir and Bengal who are non-vegetarians. On the other hand, the Brahmins of the-Deccan and Southern India have more in common so far as food is concerned with such non-Brahmins as the Gujaratis, Marwaris, Banias and Jains. There is no doubt that from the standpoint of making the transit from one caste to another easy, the fusion of the Kayasthas of Northern India and the other Non-Brahmins of Southern India with the Non-Brahmins of the Deccan and the Dravid country is more practicable than the fusion of the Brahmins of the South with the Brahmins of the North. But assuming that the fusion of sub-Castes is possible, what guarantee is there that the abolition of sub-Castes will necessarily lead to the abolition of Castes? On the contrary, it may happen that the process may stop with the abolition of sub-Castes. In that case, the abolition of sub-Castes will only help to strengthen the Castes and make them more powerful and therefore more mischievous. This remedy is therefore neither practicable nor effective and may easily prove to be a wrong remedy. Another plan of action for the abolition of Caste is to begin with inter-caste dinners. This also, in my opinion, is an inadequate remedy. There are many Castes which allow inter-dining. But it is a common experience that inter-dining has not succeeded in killing the spirit of Caste and the consciousness of Caste. I am convinced that the real remedy is inter-marriage. Fusion of blood can alone create the feeling of being kith and kin and unless this feeling of kinship, of being kindred, becomes paramount the separatist feeling—the feeling of being aliens—created by Caste will not vanish. Among the Hindus inter-marriage must necessarily be a factor of greater force in social life than it need be in the life of the non-Hindus. Where society is already well-knit by other ties, marriage is an ordinary incident of life. But where society cut asunder, marriage as a binding force becomes a matter of urgent necessity. *The real remedy for breaking Caste is inter-marriage. Nothing else will serve as the solvent of Caste.* Your Jat-Pat-Todak Mandal has adopted this line of attack.

It is a direct and frontal attack, and I congratulate you upon a collect diagnosis and more upon your having shown the courage to tell the Hindus what is really wrong with them. Political tyranny is nothing compared to social tyranny and a reformer, who defies society, is a much more courageous man than a politician, who defies Government. You are right in holding that Caste will cease to be an operative farce only when inter-dining and inter-marriage have become matters of common course. You have located the source of the disease. But is your prescription the right prescription for the disease? Ask yourselves this question; Why is it that a large majority of Hindus do not inter-dine and do not inter-marry? Why is it that your cause is not popular? There can be only one answer to this question and it is that inter-dining and inter-marriage are repugnant to the beliefs and dogmas which the Hindus regard as sacred. Caste is not a physical object like a wall of bricks or a line of barbed wire which prevents the Hindus from co-mingling and which has, therefore, to be pulled down. Caste is a notion, it is a state of the mind. The destruction of Caste does not therefore mean the destruction of a physical barrier. It means a *notional* change. Caste may be bad. Caste may lead to conduct so gross as to be called man's inhumanity to man. All the same, it must be recognized that the Hindus observe Caste not because they are inhuman or wrong headed. They observe Caste because they are deeply religious. People are not wrong in observing Caste. In my view, what is wrong is their religion, which has inculcated this notion of Caste. If this is correct, then obviously the enemy, you must grapple with, is not the people who observe Caste, but the *Shastras* which teach them this religion of Caste. Criticising and ridiculing people for not inter-dining or inter-marrying or occasionally holding inter-caste dinners and celebrating inter-caste marriages, is a futile method of achieving the desired end. The real remedy is to destroy the belief in the sanctity of the *Shastras*. How do you expect to succeed, if you allow the *Shastras* to continue to mould the beliefs and opinions of the people? Not to question the authority of the *Shastras*, to permit the people to believe in their sanctity and their sanctions and to blame them and to criticise them for their acts as being irrational and inhuman is a incongruous way of carrying on social reform. Reformers working for the removal of untouchability including Mahatma Gandhi, do not seem to realize that the acts of the people are merely the results of their beliefs inculcated upon their minds by the *Shastras* and that people will not change their conduct until they cease to believe in the sanctity of the *Shastras* on which their conduct is founded.

232   *Dalit Freedom — Now and Forever*

No wonder that such efforts have not produced any results. You also seem to be erring in the same way as the reformers working in the cause of removing untouchability. To agitate for and to organise inter-caste dinners and inter-caste marriages is like forced feeding brought about by artificial means. Make every man and woman free from the thraldom of the *Shastras*, cleanse their minds of the pernicious notions founded on the *Shastras*, and he or she will inter-dine and inter-marry, without your telling him or her to do so.

It is no use seeking refuge in quibbles. It is no use telling people that the *Shastras* do not say what they are believed to say, grammatically read or logically interpreted. What matters is how the *Shastras* have been understood by the people. You must take the stand that Buddha took. You must take the stand which Guru Nanak took. You must not only discard the *Shastras*, you must deny their authority, as did Buddha and Nanak. You must have courage to tell the Hindus, that what is wrong with them is their religion— the religion which has produced in them this notion of the sacredness of Caste. Will you show that courage?

XXI

What are your chances of success? Social reforms fall into different species. There is a species of reform, which does not relate to the religious notion of people but is purely secular in character. There is also a species of reform, which relates to the religious notions of people. Of such a species of reform, there are two varieties. In one, the reform accords with the principles of the religion and merely invites people, who have departed from it, to revert to them and to follow them. The second is a reform which not only touches the religious principles but is diametrically opposed to those principles and invites people to depart from and to discard their authority and to act contrary to those principles. Caste is the natural outcome of certain religious beliefs which have the sanction of the *Shastras,* which are believed to contain the command of divinely inspired sages who were endowed with a supernatural wisdom and whose commands, therefore, cannot be disobeyed without committing sin. The destruction of Caste is a reform which falls under the third category. To ask people to give up Caste is to ask them to go contrary to their fundamental religious notions. It is obvious that the first and second species of reform are easy. But the third is a stupendous task, well nigh impossible. The Hindus hold to the sacredness of the social order. Caste has a divine basis. You must therefore destroy the sacredness and divinity with which Caste has become invested. In the last analysis, this means you must destroy the authority of the *Shastras* and the *Vedas.*

I have emphasized this question of the ways and means of destroying Caste, because I think that knowing the proper ways and means is more important than knowing the ideal. If you do not know the real ways and means, all your shots are sure to be misfires. If my analysis is correct then your task is herculean. You alone can say whether you are capable of achieving it.

Speaking for myself, I see the task to be well nigh impossible. Perhaps you would like to know why I think so. Out of the many reasons, which have led me to take this view, I will mention some, which I regard much important. One of these reasons is the attitude of hostility, which the Brahmins have shown towards this question. The Brahmins form the vanguard of the movement for political reform and in some cases also of economic reform. But they are not to be found even as camp followers in the army raised to break down the barricades of Caste. Is there any hope of the Brahmins ever taking up a lead in the future in this matter? I say no. You may ask why? You may argue that there is no reason why Brahmins should continue to shun social reform. You may argue that the Brahmins know that the bane of Hindu Society is Caste and as an enlightened class could not be expected to be indifferent to its consequences. You may argue that there are secular Brahmins and priestly Brahmins and if the latter do not take up the cudgels on behalf of those who want to break Caste, the former will. All this of course sounds very plausible. But in all this it is forgotten that the break up of the Caste system is bound to affect adversely the Brahmin Caste. Having regard to this, is it reasonable to expect that the Brahmins will ever consent to lead a movement the ultimate result of which is to destroy the power and prestige of the Brahmin Caste? Is it reasonable to expect the secular Brahmins to take part in a movement directed against the priestly Brahmins? In my judgment, it is useless to make a distinction between the secular Brahmins and priestly Brahmins. Both are kith and kin. They are two arms of the same body and one bound to fight for the existence of the other. In this connection, I am reminded of some very pregnant remarks made by Prof. Dicey in his *English Constitution.* Speaking of the actual limitation on the legislative supremacy of Parliament, Dicey says: " The actual exercise of authority by any sovereign whatever, and notably by Parliament, is bounded or controlled by two limitations. Of these the one is an external, and the other is an internal limitation. The external limit to the real power of a sovereign consists in the possibility or certainty that his subjects or a large number of them will disobey or resist his laws. . . The internal limit to the exercise of sovereignty arises from the nature of the sovereign power itself. Even a despot exercises his powers in accordance with his character, which is itself moulded by the circumstance under which he lives, including under that head the moral feelings of the time and the society to which he belongs. The

Sultan could not, if he would, change the religion of the Mohammedan world, but even if he could do so, it is in the very highest degree improbable that the head of Mohammedanism should wish to overthrow the religion of Mohammed; the internal check on the exercise of the Sultan's power is at least as strong as the external limitation. People sometimes ask the idle question, why the Pope does not introduce this or that reform? The true answer is that a revolutionist is not the kind of man who becomes a Pope and that a man who becomes a Pope has no wish to be a revolutionist." I think, these remarks apply equally to the Brahmins of India and one can say with equal truth that if a man who becomes a Pope has no wish to become a revolutionary, a man who is born a Brahmin has much less desire to become a revolutionary. Indeed, to expect a Brahmin to be a revolutionary in matters of social reform is as idle as to expect the British Parliament, as was said by Leslie Stephen, to pass an Act requiring all blue-eyed babies to be murdered.

Some of you will say that it is a matter of small concern whether the Brahmins come forward to lead the movement against Caste or whether they do not. To take this view is in my judgment to ignore the part played by the intellectual class in the community. Whether you accept the theory of the great man as the maker of history or whether you do not, this much you will have to concede that in every country the intellectual class is the most influential class, if not the governing class. The intellectual class is the class which can foresee, it is the class which can advise and give lead. In no country does the mass of the people live the life of intelligent thought and action. It is largely imitative and follows the intellectual class. There is no exaggeration in saying that the entire destiny of a country depends upon its intellectual class. If the intellectual class is honest, independent and disinterested it can be trusted to take the initiative and give a proper lead when a crisis arises. It is true that intellect by itself is no virtue. It is only a means and the use of means depends upon the ends which an intellectual person pursues. An intellectual man can be a good man but he can easily be a rogue. Similarly an intellectual class may be a band of high-souled persons, ready to help, ready to emancipate erring humanity or it may easily be a gang of crooks or a body of advocates of a narrow clique from which it draws its support. You may think it a pity that the intellectual class in India is simply another name for the Brahmin caste. You may regret that the two are one.; that the existence of the intellectual class should be bound with one single caste, that this intellectual class should share the interest and the aspirations of that Brahmin caste, which has regarded itself the custodian of the interest of that caste, rather than of the interests of the country. All this may be very regrettable. But the fact remains, that the Brahmins form the intellectual class of the Hindus. It is not only an intellectual class but it is a class which is held in great reverence by the rest of the Hindus. The Hindus are taught that the Brahmins are *Bhudevas* (Gods on earth)   *vernanam brahmnam guruh !:* The Hindus are taught that Brahmins alone can be their teachers. Manu says, "If it be asked how it should be with respect to points of the Dharma which have not been specially mentioned, the answer is that which Brahmins who are Shishthas propound shall doubtless have legal force." :

ANAMNATESHU DHARMEHU KATHAM SYADITI CHEDBHVETA !
YAM SHISHTA BRAHNAM BRUYUH SA DHARMAH SYADASHNKITAH !!

When such an intellectual class, which holds the rest of the community in its grip, is opposed to the reform of Caste, the chances of success in a movement for the break-up of the Caste system appear to me very, very remote.

The second reason, why I say the task is impossible, will be clear if you will bear in mind that the Caste system has two aspects. In one of its aspects, it divides men into separate communities. In its second aspect, it places these communities in a graded order one above the other in social status. Each caste takes its pride and its consolation in the fact that in the scale of castes it is above some other caste. As an outward mark of this gradation, there is also a gradation of social and religious rights technically spoken of an *Ashta-dhikaras* and *Sanskaras*. The higher the grade of a caste, the greater the number of these rights and the lower the grade, the lesser their number. Now this gradation, this scaling of castes, makes it impossible to organise a common front against the Caste System. If a caste claims the right to inter-dine and inter-marry with another caste placed above it, it is frozen, instantly it is told by mischief-mongers, and there are many Brahmins amongst such mischief-mongers, that it will have to concede inter-dining and inter-marriage with castes below it ! All are slaves of the Caste System. But all the slaves are not equal in status. To excite the proletariat to bring about an economic revolution, Karl Marx told them: " You have nothing to lose except your chains." But the artful way in which the social and religious rights are distributed among the different castes whereby some have more and some have less, makes the slogan of Karl Marx quite useless to excite the Hindus against the Caste System. Castes form a graded system of sovereignties, high and low, which are jealous of their status and which know that if a general dissolution came, some of them stand to lose more of their prestige and power than others do. You cannot, therefore, have a general mobilization of the Hindus, to use a military expression, for an attack on the Caste System.

XXII

Can you appeal to reason and ask the Hindus to discard Caste as being contrary to reason? That raises the question: Is a Hindu free to follow his reason? Manu has laid down three sanctions to which every Hindu must conform in the matter of his behaviour *vedah smritih sadacharah uvasy cha priyamatmanah* Here there is no place for reason to play its part. A Hindu must follow either *Veda, Smriti* or *Sadachar.* He cannot follow anything else. In the first place how are the texts of the *Vedas* and *Smritis* to be interpreted whenever any doubt arises regarding their meaning? On this important question the view of Manu is quite definite. He says :

YOVAMANYET TE MOOLE HETUSHRASHRAYA DWIZAH

SA SADHUBHIRBAHISHKARYO NASHTIKO VEDANDIKAH

According to this rule, rationalism as a canon of interpreting the *Vedas* and *Smritis,* is absolutely condemned. It is regarded to be as wicked as atheism and the punishment provided for it is ex-communication. Thus, where a matter is covered by the *Veda* or the *Smriti,* a Hindu cannot resort to rational thinking. Even when there is a conflict between *Vedas* and *Smritis* on matters on which they have given a positive injunction, the solution is not left to reason. When there is a conflict between two *Shrutis,* both are to be regarded as of equal authority. Either of them may be followed. No attempt is to be made to find out which of the two accords with reason. This is made clear by *Manu:*

SHRUTIDWADHAM TU YATRA SYAPTATRA DHARVARVUDHAU SMRITAU

"When there is a conflict between *Shruti and Sinriti,* the *Shruti* must prevail." But here too, no attempt must be made to find out which of the two accords with reason. This is laid down by Manu in the following Shloka :

YA VEDABAHYAH SNRITYO YASHCH KASHCH
KRIDRISHTAH I
SARVASTA NISHPHALAH PRETY TAMONISHTHA HI
TAH SMRITAH II

Again, when there is a conflict between two *Smritis*, the Manu-Smriti must prevail, but no attempt is to be made to find out which of the two accords with reason. This is the ruling given by Brihaspati:

VEDAYATVOPANIBANDHRITAVAT PRAMANYAM
HI MANOAH SMRITAH
MANVRTHAVIPARITA TU YA SMRITIH SA NA
SHASHYATE

It is, therefore, clear that in any matter on which the *Shrutis* and *Smritis* have given a positive direction, a Hindu is not free to use his reasoning faculty. The same rule is laid down in the Mahabharat :

PURANAM MANVO DHARMAH SANGO
VEDASHCHIKITSITAM
AGASIDHANI CHATVARI NA HANTAVYANI
HETUBHIH

He must abide by their directions. The Caste and *Varna* are matters, which are dealt with by the *Vedas* and the *Smritis* and consequently, appeal to reason can have no effect on a Hindu. So far as Caste and *Varna* are concerned, not only the *Shastras* do not permit the Hindu to use his reason in the decision of the question, but they have taken care to see that no occasion is left to examine in a rational way the foundations of his belief in Caste and *Varna*. It must be a source of silent amusement to many a Non-Hindu to find hundreds and thousands of Hindus breaking Caste on certain occasions, such as railway journey and foreign travel and yet endeavouring to maintain Caste for the rest of their lives ! The explanation of this phenomenon discloses another fetter on the reasoning faculties of the Hindus. Man's life is generally habitual and unreflective. Reflective thought, in the sense of active, persistent and careful consideration of any belief or supposed form or knowledge in the light of the grounds that support it and further conclusions to which it tends, is quite rare and arises only in a situation which presents a dilemma – a Crisis-Railway journeys and foreign travels are really occasions of crisis in the life of a Hindu and it is natural to expect a Hindu to ask himself why he should maintain Caste at all, if he cannot maintain it at all times. But he does not. He breaks Caste at one step and proceeds to observe it at the next without raising any question. The reason for this astonishing conduct is to be found in the rule of the *Shastras*, which directs him to maintain Caste as far as possible and to undergo *praynschitia* when he cannot. By this theory of *prayaschitta*, the *Shastras* by following a spirit of compromise have given caste a perpetual lease of life and have smothered reflective thought which would have otherwise led to the destruction of the notion of Caste.

There have been many who have worked in the cause of the abolition of Caste and Untouchability. Of those, who can be mentioned, Ramanuja, Kabir and others stand out prominently. Can you appeal to the acts of these reformers and exhort the Hindus to follow them? It is true that Manu has included *Sadachar (sadachar)* as one of the sanctions along with *Shruti* and *Smriti*. Indeed, *Sadachar* has been given a higher place than *Shastras* :

> *YADDWACHARYATE YEN DHARMYA*
> *VADHARMAMEV VA*
> *DESHASYACHARANAM NITYAM CHARITRAM*
> *TADWIKIRTATAM*

According to this, *sadachar*, whether, it is *dharmy*a or *adharmy*a in accordance with *Shastras* or contrary to *Shastras*, must be followed. But what is the meaning of *Sadachar*? If any one were to suppose that *Sadachar* means right or good acts *i.e.* acts of good and righteous men he would find himself greatly mistaken. *Sadachar* does not means good acts or acts of good men. It means ancient custom *good* or *bad*. The following verse makes this clear :

YASMIN DESHE YA ACHARAH
PARMPAYAKRAMAGATAH
VARNANI KIL SARVESHAM SA SADACHAR
UCHYATE

As though to warn people against the view that *Sadachar* means good *acts* or acts of good men and fearing that people might understand it that way and follow the acts of good men, the *Smrities* have commanded the Hindus in unmistakable terms not to follow even Gods in their good deeds, if they are contrary to *Shruti, Smrili* and *Sadachar*. This may sound to be most extraordinary, most perverse, but the. fact remains that *na devacharitam charet* is an injunction, issued to the Hindus by their *Shastras*. Reason and morality are the two most powerful weapons in the armoury of a Reformer. To deprive him of the use of these weapons is to disable him for action .How are you going to break up Caste, if people are not free to consider whether it accords with reason? How are you going to break up Caste if people are not free to consider whether it accords with morality? The wall built around Caste is impregnable and the material, of which it is built, contains none of the combustible stuff of reason and morality. Add to this the fact that inside this wall stands the army of Brahmins, who form the intellectual class, Brahmins who are the natural leaders of the Hindus, Brahmins who are there not as mere mercenary soldiers but as an army fighting for its homeland and you will get an idea why I think that breaking-up of Caste amongst the Hindus is well-nigh impossible. At any rate, it would take ages before a breach is made. But whether the doing of the deed takes time or whether it can be *done* quickly, you must not forget that if you wish to bring about & breach in the system then you have got to apply the dynamite to the *Vedas* and the *Shastras,* which deny any part to reason, to *Vedas* and *Shastras,* which deny any part to morality. You must destroy the Religion of the *Shrutis* and the *Smritis.* Nothing else will avail. This is my considered view of the matter.

XXIII

Some may not understand what I mean by destruction of Religion; some may find the idea revolting to them and some may find it revolutionary. Let me therefore explain my position. I do not know whether you draw a distinction between principles and rules. But I do. Not only I make a distinction but I say that this distinction is real and important. Rules are practical; they are habitual ways of doing things according to prescription. But principles are intellectual; they are useful methods of judging things. Rules seek to tell an agent just what course of action to pursue. Principles do not prescribe a specific course of action. Rules, like cooking recipes, do tell just what to do and how to do it. A principle, such as that of justice, supplies a main head by reference to which he is to consider the bearings of his desires and purposes, it guides him in his thinking by suggesting to him the important consideration which he should bear in mind. This difference between rules and principles makes the acts done in pursuit of them different in quality and in content. Doing what is said to *be,* good by virtue of a rule and doing good in the light of a principle are two different things. The principle may be wrong but the act is conscious and responsible. The rule may be right but the act is mechanical. A religious act may not be a correct act but must at least be a responsible act. To permit of this responsibility, Religion must mainly *be* a matter of principles only. It cannot be a matter of rules. The moment it degenerates into rules it ceases to be Religion, as it kills responsibility which is the essence of a truly religious act. What is this Hindu Religion? Is it a set of principles or is it a code of rules? Now the Hindu Religion, as contained in the *Vedas* and the *Smritis*, is nothing but a mass of sacrificial, social, political and sanitary rules and regulations, all mixed up. What is called Religion by the Hindus is nothing but a multitude of commands and prohibitions. Religion, in the sense of spiritual principles, truly universal, applicable to all races, to all countries, to all times, is not to be found in them, and if it is, it does not form the governing part of a Hindu's life. That for a Hindu, Dharma means commands and prohibitions is clear from the way the word Dharma is used in *Vedas* and the *Sinritis* and understood by the commentators. The word Dharma as used in the *Vedas* in most cases means religious ordinances or rites. Even Jaimini in his Purva-Mimansa defines Dharma as "a desirable goal or result that is indicated by injunctive *(Vedic)* passages ". To put it in plain language, what the Hindus call Religion is really Law or at best legalized class-ethics. Frankly, I refuse to cull this code of ordinances, as Religion. The first evil of such a code of ordinances, misrepresented to the people as Religion, is that it tends to deprive moral life of freedom and spontaneity and to reduce it (for the conscientious at any rate) to a *more* or less anxious and servile conformity to externally imposed rules. Under it, there is no loyalty to ideals, there is only conformity to commands. But the worst evil of this code of ordinances is that the laws it contains must be the same yesterday, today and forever. They are iniquitous in that they are not the same for one class as for another. But this iniquity is made perpetual in that they are prescribed to be the same for all generations. The objectionable part of such a scheme is not that they are made by certain persons called Prophets or Law-givers. The objectionable part is that this code has been invested with the character of finality and fixity. Happiness notoriously varies with the conditions and circumstances of a person, as well as with the conditions of different people and epochs. That being the case, how can humanity endure this code of eternal laws, without being cramped and without being crippled? I have, therefore, no hesitation in saying that such a religion must be destroyed and I say, there is nothing irreligious in working for the destruction of such a religion. Indeed I hold that it is your bounden duty to tear the mask, to remove the misrepresentation that as caused by misnaming this Law as Religion. This is an essential step for you. Once you clear the minds of the people of this misconception and enable them to realize that what they are told as Religion is not Religion but that it is really Law, you will be in a position to urge for its amendment or abolition. So long as people look upon it as Religion they will not be ready for a change, because the idea of Religion is generally speaking not associated with the idea of change. But the idea of law is associated with the idea of change and when people come to know that what is called Religion is really Law, old and archaic, they will be ready for a change, for people know and accept that law can be changed.

XXIV   While I condemn a Religion of Rules, I must not be understood to hold the opinion that there is no necessity for a religion. On the contrary, I agree with Burke when he says that, " True religion is the foundation of society, the basis on which all true Civil Government rests, and both their sanction." Consequently, when I urge that these ancient rules of life be annulled, I am anxious that its place shall be taken by a Religion of Principles, which alone can lay claim to being a true Religion. Indeed, I am so convinced of the necessity of Religion that I feel I ought to tell you in outline what I regard as necessary items in this religious reform. The following in my opinion should be the cardinal items in this reform: (1) There should be one and only one standard book of Hindu Religion, acceptable to all Hindus and recognized by all Hindus. This of course means that all other books of Hindu religion such as *Vedas, Shastras* and *Puranas,* which are treated as sacred and authoritative, must by law cease to be so and the preaching of any doctrine, religious or social contained in these books should be penalized. (2) It should be better if priesthood among Hindus was abolished. But as this seems to be impossible, the priesthood must at least cease to be hereditary. Every person who professes to be a Hindu must be eligible for being a priest. It should be provided by law that no Hindu shall be entitled to be a priest unless he has passed an examination prescribed by the State and holds a *sanad* from the State permitting him to practise. (3) No ceremony performed by a priest who does not hold a *sanad* shall be deemed to be valid in law and it should be made penal for a person who has no *sanad* to officiate as a priest. (4) A priest should be the servant of the State and should be subject to the disciplinary action by the State in the matter of his morals, beliefs and worship, in addition to his being subject along with other citizens to the ordinary law of the land. (5) The number of priests should be limited by law according to the requirements of the State as is done in the case of the I.C.S. To some, this may sound radical. But to my mind there is nothing revolutionary in this. Every profession in India is regulated. Engineers must show proficiency, Doctor must show proficiency, Lawyers must show proficiency, before they are allowed to practise their professions. During the whole of their career, they must not only obey the law of the land, civil as well as criminal, but they must also obey the special code of morals prescribed by their respective professions. The priest's is the only profession where proficiency is not required. The profession of a Hindu priest is the only profession which is not subject to any code. Mentally a priest may be an idiot, physically a priest may be suffering from a foul disease, such as syphilis or gonorrheae, morally he may be a wreck. But he is fit to officiate at solemn ceremonies, to enter the *sanctum sanctorum* of a Hindu temple and worship the Hindu God. All this becomes possible among the Hindus because for a priest it is enough to be born in a priestly caste. The whole thing is abominable and is due to the fact that the priestly class among Hindus is subject neither to law nor to morality. It recognizes no duties. It knows only of rights and privileges. It is a pest which divinity seems to have let loose on the masses for their mental and moral degradation. The priestly class must be brought under control by some such legislation as I have outlined above. It will prevent it from doing mischief and from misguiding people. It will democratise it by throwing it open to every one. It will certainly help to kill the Brahminism and will also help to kill Caste, which is nothing but Brahminism incarnate. Brahminism is the poison which has spoiled Hinduism. You will succeed in saving Hinduism if you will kill Brahminism. There should be no opposition to this reform from any quarter. It should be welcomed even by the Arya Samajists, because this is merely an application of their own doctrine of *guna-karma*.

Whether you do that or you do not, you must give a new doctrinal basis to your Religion—a basis that will be in consonance with Liberty, Equality and Fraternity, in short, with Democracy. I am no authority on the subject. But I am told that for such religious principles as will be in consonance with Liberty, Equality and Fraternity it may not be necessary for you to borrow from foreign sources and that you could draw for such principles on the *Upanishads*. Whether you could do so without a complete remoulding, a considerable scraping and chipping off the ore they contain, is more than I can say. This means a complete change in the fundamental notions of life-it means a complete change in the values of life. It means a complete change in outlook and in attitude towards men and things. It means conversion but if you do not. like the word, I will say, it means new life. But a new life cannot enter a body that is dead. New life can center only in a new body. The old body must die before a new body can come into existence and a new life can enter into it. To put it simply: the old must cease to be operative before the new can begin to enliven and to pulsate. This is what I meant when I said you must discard the authority of the *Shastras* and destroy the religion of the *Shastras*.

XXV

I have kept you too long. It is time I brought this address to a close. This would have been a convenient point for me to have stopped. But this would probably be my last address to a Hindu audience on a subject vitally concerning the Hindus. I would therefore like, before I close, to place before the Hindus, if they will allow me, some questions which I regard as vital and invite them seriously to consider the same.

In the first place, the Hindus must consider whether it is sufficient to take the placid view of the anthropologist that there is nothing to be said about the beliefs, habits, morals and outlooks on life, which obtain among the different peoples of the world except that they often differ; or whether it is not necessary to make an attempt to find out what kind of morality, beliefs, habits and outlook have worked best and have enabled those who possessed them to flourish, *to* go strong, to people the earth and to have dominion over it. As is observed by Prof. Carver, "

Morality and religion, as the organised expression of moral approval and disapproval, must be regarded as factors in the struggle for existence as truly as are weapons for offence and defence, teeth and claws, horns and hoofs, furs and feathers. The social group, community, tribe or nation, which develops an unworkable scheme of morality or within which those social acts which weaken it and unfit it for survival, habitually create the sentiment of approval, while those which would strengthen and enable it to be expanded habitually create the sentiment of disapproval, will eventually be eliminated. It is its habits of approval or disapproval (these are the results of religion and morality) that handicap it, as really as the possession of two wings on one side with none on. the other will handicap the colony of flies. It would be as futile in the one case as in the other to argue, that one system is just as good as another." Morality and religion, therefore, are not mere matters of likes and dislikes. You may dislike exceedingly a scheme of morality, which, if universally practised within a nation, would make that nation the strongest nation on the face of the earth. Yet in spite of your dislike such a nation will become strong. You may like exceedingly a scheme of morality and an ideal of justice, which if universally practised within a nation, would make it enable to hold its own in the struggle with other nations. Yet in spite of your admiration this nation will eventually disappear. The Hindus must, therefore, examine their religion and then morality in terms of their survival value.

Secondly, the Hindus must consider whether they should conserve the whole of their social heritage or select what is helpful and transmit to future generations only that much and no more. Prof, John Dewey., who was my teacher and to whom I owe so much, has said: " Every society gets encumbered with what is trivial, with dead wood from the past, and with what is positively perverse... As a society becomes more enlightened, it realizes that it is responsible *not* to conserve and transmit, the whole of its existing achievements, but only such as make for a better future society." Even Burke in spite of the vehemence with which he opposed the principle of change embodied in the French Revolution, was compelled to admit that " a State without the means of some change is without the means of its conservation. Without such means it might even risk the loss of that part of the constitution which it wished the most religiously to preserve, " What Burke said of a State applies equally to a society.

Thirdly, the Hindus must consider whether they must not cease to worship the past as supplying its ideals. The beautiful effect of this worship of the past are best summed up by Prof. Dewey when he says: " An individual can live only in the present. The present is not just something which comes after the past; much less something produced by it. It is what life is in leaving the past behind it. The study of past products will not help us to understand the present. A knowledge of the past and its heritage is of great significance when it enters into the present, but not otherwise. And the mistake of making the-records and remains of the past the main material of education is that it tends to make the past a rival of the present and the present a more or less futile imitation of the past." The principle, which makes little of the present act of living and growing, naturally looks upon the present as empty and upon the future as remote. Such a principle is inimical to progress and is an hindrance to a strong and a steady current of life.

Fourthly, the Hindus must consider whether the time has not come for them to recognize that there is nothing fixed, nothing eternal, nothing *sanatan;* that everything is changing, that change is the law of life for individuals as well as for society. In a changing society, there must be a constant revolution of old values and the Hindus must realize that if there must be standards to measure the acts of men there must also be a readiness to revise those standards.

XXVI

I have to confess that this address has become too lengthy. Whether this fault is compensated to any extent by breadth or depth is a matter for you to judge. All I claim is to have told you candidly my views. I have little to recommend them but some study and a deep concern in your destiny. If you will allow me to say, *these* views are the views of a man, who has been no tool of power, no flatterer of greatness. They come from one, almost the whole of whose public exertion has been one continuous struggle for liberty for the poor and for the oppressed and whose only reward has been a continuous shower of calumny and abuse from national journals and national leaders, for no other reason except that I refuse to join with them in performing the miracle — I will not say trick — of liberating the oppressed with the gold of the tyrant and raising the poor with the cash of the rich. All this may not be enough to commend my views. I think they are not likely to alter yours. But whether they do or do not, the responsibility is entirely yours. You must make your efforts to uproot Caste, if not in my way, then in your way. I am sorry, I will not be with you. I have decided to change. This is not the place for giving reasons. But even when I am gone out of your fold, I will watch your movement with active sympathy and you will have my assistance for what it may be worth. Yours is a national cause. Caste is no doubt primarily the breath of the Hindus. But the Hindus have fouled the air all over and everybody is infected, Sikh, Muslim and Christian. You, therefore, deserve the support of all those who are suffering from this infection, Sikh, Muslim and Christian. Yours is more difficult than the other national cause, namely Swaraj. In the fight for Swaraj you fight with the whole nation on your side. In this, you have to fight against the whole nation and that too, your own. But it is more important than Swaraj. There is no use having Swaraj, if you cannot defend it. More important than the question of defending Swaraj is the question of defending the Hindus under the Swaraj. In my opinion only when the Hindu Society becomes a casteless society that it can hope to have strength enough to defend itself. Without such internal strength, Swaraj for Hindus may turn out to be only a step towards slavery. Good-bye and good wishes for your success.

Selected References

Chandra, Ramesh (ed.), <u>Dalits and the Ideology of Revolt</u>, New Delhi: Common Wealth Publisher, 2003.

Chandra, Ramesh (ed.), <u>Dalit Identity in the New Millennium</u>, Vol. 1-10, New Delhi: Commonwealth Publishers, 2003.

Chandra, Ramesh (ed.), <u>Dalits and their Future</u>, New Delhi: Common Wealth, 2003.

Chandra, Ramesh, <u>Phases of Dalit Revolt</u>, New Delhi: Commonwealth Publishers, 2003.

Chaudhary, S.N., <u>Dalit and Tribal Leadership in Panchayats</u>, New Delhi: Concept Publishing company, 2004.

D., Manohar Chandra Prasad, <u>Broken God Broken People: The Plight of Dalit Christians</u>, Bangalore: Rachana Publications, 1996.

Das, K.C, <u>Indian Dalits</u>, Delhi: Global Vision Publishing House, 2004.

Devasahayam, V., <u>Doing Dalit Theology in Biblical Key</u>, Madras: Gurukul, 1997.

Devasahayam, V., Frontiers of Dalit Theology, Madras: Gurukul, 1997.

Deulkar, Sita, Dalits Past, Present and Future, New Delhi: Dominant Publishers, 2004.

Doniger, Wendy and Brian K. Smith, The Laws of Manu, New Delhi: Penguin, 1991.

Dalitology: The Book of the Dalit People, Tumkur: Ambedkar Resource Center, 2003

Dr. Babasaheb Ambedkar Writing and Speeches, Vol. 1-8, Bombay: Education Department of Government of Maharashtra, 1982.

Fernandes, Walter, The Emerging Dalit Identity: The Re-Assertion of the Subalterns, New Delhi: Indian Social Institute, 1996.

Ghosh, G.K., Dalit Women, New Delhi: A.P.H. Publishing Corporation, 1997.

Human Rights Watch, Broken People, New York: Books for Change, 1999.

Irudayaraj, Xavier (ed.), Emerging Dalit Theology, Madras: JEST: TTS, 1990.

Kumar, Vijendra, Rise of Dalit Power in India, Jaipur: ABD Publisher.

Lal, A.K., Dalit in Action, New Delhi: Concept Publication,1997.

Madan, G.R, <u>Casteism Corruption And Social Development in India</u>, New Delhi: Radha publication, 2004.

Mathew P. D., <u>Constitution of India</u>, New Delhi: Indian Social Institute, 1996.

Michael, S.M. (ed.), <u>Dalits in Modern India</u>: Vision and Values, New Delhi: Vistaar Publication, 1999.

Mohanty, R.P., <u>Dalits Development and Change</u>, New Delhi: Discover Publishing House, 2003.

Nirmal, P. Arvind, <u>A Reader in Dalit Theology</u>, Madras: Gurukul Lutheran Theological College and Research Institute, n.d.

Nirmal, P. Arvind, <u>Towards A Common Dalit Ideology</u>, Madras: Gurukul Lutheran Theological College and Research Institute, n.d.

Paswan, Sanjay (ed.), <u>Encyclopaedia of Dalits in India</u>, Vol. 1-11, Delhi: Kalpaz Publication, 2002.

Prabhakar, M. E. (ed.), <u>Towards A Dalit Theology</u>, Delhi: ISPCK, 1989.

Prakash, Surendra, <u>Concise Manu Smrti</u>, Delhi: CIRSR, 2000.

Prasad, Ravi, D. M, <u>Dalit Youth</u>: A Sociological Study, New Delhi: APH Publishing Corporations, 1997.

Puri, Harish. K., <u>Dalits in Regional Context</u>, Jaipur: Rawat Publication, 2004.

Pylee, M. V., An Introduction To The Constitution of India, New Delhi: Vikas, 1995.

Samuel, Swapna H., Dalit Movement in South India, (1857-1950), New Delhi: Serial Publications, 2004.

Shah, Ghanshyam (ed.), Dalits and the State, New Delhi: Concept Publishing, 2002.

Singh, Buta, The Dalits and Dalit Awakening in India, New Delhi; Gyan Publishing House, 2004.

Singh, Mahender, Dalits in India, New Delhi: Reference Press, 2003.

Sivaprakasam, M.V., Dalits and Social Mobilization, New Delhi: Rajat Publications, 2002.

Tripathy, Rebati Ballav, Dalits: A Sub-Human Society, New Delhi: Ashish Publishing House, 1994.

Verma, D.K. (ed.), Ambedkar Vision and Education of Weaker Sections, Delhi: Manak Publisher, 2004.

Zelliot, Eleanor, From Untouchables to Dalit: Essays on the Ambedkar Movement, New Delhi: Manohar Publisher, 2001.

About the Author

Dr. Joseph D'souza is the President of the All India Christian Council, one of the largest interdenominational alliances of Christians dealing with national and human rights issues. The Council addresses the issue of the persecution and oppression of Christians and other minorities in India. D'souza represents Indian Christians and Dalit issues in the media and other national and international forums. The All India Christian Council is affiliated with Christian Solidarity Worldwide of which D'souza has served as the International President.

D'souza is also the International President of the Dalit Freedom Network and the Associate International Director of OM International. D'souza focuses on issues of freedom of religion and human rights. He travels extensively in his campaign for the rights of the oppressed and marginalized in society, especially for the rights of the Dalits and the Backward Castes in India.

D'souza is widely quoted in the press and on major media channels like CNN and BBC, which continue to interview him on issues related to Dalit Freedom, minority rights and Hindutva.

D'souza lives in India and operates out of Hyderabad; London, England; and Denver, USA.

The Dalit Freedom Network:
Created to Empower India's Dalits

Created in 2002 in the United States, the Dalit Freedom Network's (DFN) mission is to empower the Dalits in their quest for socio-spiritual freedom and human dignity by networking human, financial and information resources.

A movement of this magnitude among India's Dalits requires an intense and lasting effort by many people worldwide to have any lasting effect. DFN is a clearinghouse of information on activities involving the Dalits. DFN has components working in strategic areas including:

- Dalit Education Centers
- Medical Supplies and Services
- Economic Development
- Advocacy and Human Rights

This international movement exists to give India's Dalits a voice to be heard socially, politically and spiritually. To do this, DFN has a central office located in Denver, Colorado, acting as the hub to connect people and finances to the areas of need in India. Its board consists of men and women from a variety of professional backgrounds. Its advisory board represents a high-profile section of American and Indian society. DFN works in a strategic partnership with the All India Christian Council.

For the first time in history, the Dalits now have a voice which can be heard socially and politically in India and around the world. DFN pledges solidarity with the AICC and with the Dalits. Together they are confident they can help bring a notable transformation that will last forever.

259

Join the cause of the Dalits today by passing on this book
or the information herein to other people.

For more information, and for additional
copies of
Dalit Freedom – Now And Forever by Joseph D'souza
contact:

DALIT FREEDOM NETWORK CANADA
#407 – 7337 – 137th Street
Surrey, BC V3W 1A4 Canada

Phone: 604-592-2238 Fax: 604-592-2239
Email: info@dalitfreedom.net
Web: www.dalitfreedom.net